Can You See

God

in This Picture?

A Letter to My Sons

Making Sense of 25 Years as a Pastor

John H. King

Can You See God in This Picture:
A Letter to My Sons
Making Sense of 25 Years as a Pastor

Published by J. Timothy King

First trade paperback edition, October 2008

Printed in the United States of America.

ISBN 978-0-9816925-1-7
ISBN-10 0-9816925-1-6

http://CanYouSeeGodInThisPicture.com/

10 9 8 7 6 5 4 3 2 1

Front cover: The Burgettstown church (see the photos in the back), drawn by one of the author's sons, at the age of 5, who also then asked the question which became the title of this work.

To my family, whom I love

Acknowledgments

I am grateful to family and friends who humored my interest in re-living memories both good and not so good. They might disagree with my interpretations and even some of my recollections but they seemed to enjoy the opportunity none-the-less to talk about it. This is huge when memories have a potential of hurt or raising unresolved issues. Not talking about it is often the preferred approach but if that had been the case these pages possibly would never have been written.

I want to especially thank my son, Tim, for his work of proof-reader. He knows the English language better than I. I tend to write as I talk in colloquialisms and slang words and phrases with which the reader might not be familiar. I bow to his judgment in such cases. He was careful not to erase my fingerprint on this work. I assure you, it is all me.

I would be amiss if I failed to thank my dear wife not so much for helping me write this story but helping me live through it. I cannot count the times she was my listening post, my silent helper, the person who had to cushion the shock of my rage when I felt someone was painfully unfair toward poor me. More ideas passed her ears that had no right to reality because they would have irreparably damaged those we loved or came to love. She sheltered me from an incalculable amount of regret. And above all and through all she had to endure, I thank her for her continuing love.

Preface

These are the thoughts of someone who once pastored churches. These thoughts are written primarily to my sons who grew up in the church. Such an experience is more often than not lacking in the beauty and meaning that God envisioned when He first called His church into being.

My ministry as a pastor and teacher spanned the years from 1969 to 1993. During this time I worked odd jobs to make ends meet: painting houses, teaching Biblical Greek, or whatever. This kind of life is very common for the clergy. Many in those days understood the concept of a vow of poverty and became dependent on the members of the local church to provide for them.

This didn't always work out to our advantage. My family and I were occasionally down to the last jar of peanut butter (never quite the bag of cornmeal), so it was believable to say God was taking care of us. Faith was a real part of our experience. If we were going to ever disown God or blame Him for anything, then was not the time.

Sometimes things didn't work out at all. February '72 we ran out of money and had to move out of our rented apartment before we were evicted. We spent three weeks in Buffalo with mother before returning to Pennsylvania and another chance at ministry. I was fired from a painting job a few months later, tried to sell vacuum cleaners briefly, and finally took a job as a custodian in the local school district.

We moved 17 times in those years. I pastored in only five churches, though. One church gave me three months discipline. Over the four years we were there, at least we brought them through the difficulty of bringing on board their first full-time pastor. They built a parsonage for us first, but we moved three times before it was ready. Being the pastor during a church parsonage building, upon reflection, is a dubious achievement at best. At the end of the discipline period, we were on to our next assignment.

Another church was on the verge of voting me out when I resigned. The difficulty for these wonderful people—and that is not sarcasm—was to transition into an age where the lines between denominations within Christianity were becoming blurred. We attempted to join or merge two separate church groups of differing worship and theology. I was credentialed in one and affiliated with the other. Try that! I can only speculate, since I am no prophet, that within a decade or so these lines will no longer exist.

Our longest stay in any one ministry was 7 years when we left for better opportunities. Leaving there was somewhat traumatic, since there is where we grew up in ministry. I little knew then that who I would become as a pastor was defined there. I would reflect back and make future decisions based on those seven years.

One church we pastored had a 150-year history in which the average stay for a pastor was only four years. Such turnover is generally the consequence of all the angry things adults do that children see and remember. It helps define the church as an undesirable place to be. We managed only two years before moving on.

During the worst of times, nothing was clear. It was all just happening, and it was up to one's theology to determine who, if anyone, was at fault.

Just a footnote: There are three justifiable reasons for a congregation to dismiss a pastor. (1) The pastor has been morally unfaithful in marriage, (2) the pastor's theology is clearly no longer Christian, or (3) the pastor has totally lost his love for ministry. None of these applied to me, if you were wondering. Likewise a pastor can justifiably want to leave. Maybe his ministry is finished there; maybe by denominational arrangement or by a Divine calling he truly senses it is time to move on. I don't think this was me either. Generally, however, none of these reasons is why the leaving actually happens. A pastor is usually simply worn out by the infighting or power struggles or some swing in the popular vote against him. This becomes a process that involves many meetings and long hours of discussion with his spouse and less sleep and misunderstood sermons and all such things as finally yield to a resignation to leave.

If I could speak in more general terms about all preachers' kids, all this up and down has an unseen and immeasurable impact on them. Children are more likely than not tossed about in the tumbler of radical change. No wonder if some come out with a spiritual concussion, where they become only vaguely familiar with a dizzying concept of God.

Salvation for someone growing up in this environment might be a twofold miracle. Not only is his salvation the same as anyone else's, but also the change in his life has to reconcile with not only his own past sins but also ours, the grown-ups. He must somehow gain a revelation of God through the smog of everything within a church that is not Christ-motivated, and unfortunately there can be a lot of smog.

How could the children see the changes happening around them and not experience these changes' bad effects? Besides, we adults were too preoccupied with our world of words to see those effects. We would not know this, perhaps, until some of our sons and daughters decided to call it quits to churches and to everything the churches represented, including (sadly) God Himself. They decided to leave for good.

Long before this, they lost interest, a fact that should have been evident in their depressed looks, their disinterested wandering gazes during church and even Sunday School, even their slouching posture. It was a wonder that a few of them didn't slide to the floor asleep!

But our children were there anyway, and we hoped something good would come of it. We theologized and believed something that was said or experienced would direct them toward good, as adults. Bring them up in the way they should go, the Scripture says, and we took it as our promise. Maybe something good did happen, or maybe it came out of those troublesome days, or maybe we are still waiting and hoping and believing for it.

So, for whatever it is worth, I can look back and sense some empathy for my sons if they discovered that church can be painfully boring or meaningless at times.

The church was never organized with them in mind. It was put together, from theology to air conditioning, for us, the grown-ups. Our sons, all the children, were brought along with us for the ride.

Well, at the time of this writing, I have been working for the past ten years outside the church, to afford some college education, to buy a home, and to play catch-up with a retirement fund. And why not? I hope to be back, though, since ministry is in my blood, as they say. After all it is my calling.

First, I need to address the past. I need to face my past experiences. Like someone entering into a second marriage, it never helps to blame a former partner and assume a second relationship will bring happiness. We fool ourselves if we do, because it won't. I need to face who I was and what I did. I cannot pretend to anticipate future ministry while carrying the same misgivings, hurts, and suspicions I once owned. I would prefer going back into ministry with an innocence that is wise, a benevolence that knows how to lead, and a knowledge of my reality that knows the difference between selfish interest and genuine awareness of the will of God. If I retire for good, directly from my programming job, so be it. The important thing is to reconcile with the past in a way that makes it more a part of my future than just a reservoir of memories. One's past, for the most part good, should feed a passion for life, not take from it.

Some of what I say here in this memoir may be offensive to some, but since I have currently no church to lose and I think God appreciates honesty, I want to say it. Few may be vaguely interested in hearing me out. But it is true of all of us that from time to time we are talking when no one is listening. So be it.

Perhaps I speak for a young minister who may read this account and appreciate the changes we observe in today's church. Just maybe those of us who have gone before as keepers of the vision may yet be recognized for more than short-lived ministries or unfulfilled dreams. Were we bridge builders, to use Will Allen Dromgoole's idea? The last two stanzas of her poem "The Bridge Builder" pictures what I am trying to say.

The builder lifted his old gray head:
"Good friend, in the path I have come," he said,
"There followeth after me today,
A youth, whose feet must pass this way.
This chasm, that has been naught to me,
To that fair-haired youth may a pitfall be.
He, too, must cross in the twilight dim;
Good friend, I am building the bridge for him."

There are countless men and women whose godly example, which includes mistakes and failures, should be paraded before us. It would embarrass them to know this, were they not humble persons who learned big lessons from falling down and getting back up again. Their accounts should be written and read to the next generation of preachers and pastors, who may otherwise never know the facts. These biographical sketches and histories do not make it to the seminary text books. They are unimaginable details. They are unknown by congregations of, yes, godly people who are ignorant even of things their own pastors lived through. They should be told.

Unfortunately, I cannot tell their stories. I can only tell my own, which is insignificant unless you multiply it by hundreds of colleagues' personal testimonials, whose stories are strikingly similar. I know of some.

The church is changing. An introduction to my thoughts may not be the place to note the difference between then and now, but anyone who has seen both knows of these changes.

Perhaps, I speak for the minister whose congregation is slow to catch up with today's ministries. He might agree with me that some of these changes are good. Maybe he can glean encouragement from this account, or maybe an idea or two of how to endure. The church is changing. Overhead projections are common, and organs are not. The choruses sung are more universal and less the product of one style of worship. Clergy across denominations are meeting for prayer and planning things together. Churches are changing their corporate names to neutralize the old impression that they are denominational in practice. They claim to be more community-oriented. And on and on we could note the differences.

I can relate to the people who grew up in the church and left at first chance, disillusioned and disgusted with what they experienced and observed. Things that should never have happened in front of them did happen.

I will not address criminal issues. There were a few individuals who abused the pulpit by bringing lifelong harm to the children they met. Some of these clergy have been tried, found guilty, and imprisoned, and rightly so. Here we talk only of honest clergy, with whom I hope to be counted, who made mistakes in a real effort to care about their congregations, and about the congregations who sometimes retaliated in kind.

Some things I cannot say, because although this is intended to be self-revealing, it is not intended to show the possible bad side of anyone else, and everyone has a bad side. Some of what I did or didn't do, say or didn't say, probably needs psychoanalysis or something and isn't easily explained. When one church decided not to keep us because they felt I needed psychological help, leaving was imperative. But how could the reason possibly be clear enough for a non-professional like me to explain? (Though I did see a counselor for depression.)

Some things I won't say because they don't expound on what I am trying to say about myself and what made me tick as a minister.

And I suppose all of us have a human side that doesn't need mentioning. Because it is generally true of all of us, so I do not need to stand up and shout the obvious. I do not need to invite you into the private world of my thoughts just to let you know that some of them weren't so nice. You guessed that already, so why embarrass me into saying it?

I may take a certain calculated risk and say some things that could be misinterpreted or misunderstood. Some people always think the worst. But some things are worth saying.

I write this to suggest that God does heal the broken-hearted. God will yet clarify to those who left the church what His church failed to show them, that He is real and that He is capable of communicating and keeping His promises to them. My hope is that many will find their way back to Him.

Perhaps I speak for the people who attended church because they believed in God and His salvation and genuinely wanted to know Him. They never came into the church to be part of some split or breakup, but they were there when it happened and hoped they had no part in it. They were and remain honest folk who only wanted to be part of a loving Christian community, and they could not begin to explain what happened. They may need to know that everything is going to be alright. God is a God of restoration. Maybe they can see that in some way in these pages.

I write this, again, primarily—and if truth be told, in all honesty, simply—to my three sons. They know a lot. They have seen a lot. They were there through each move, each change, each challenge, each struggle their mother and I dealt with. I hope I can finally in looking back make some sense out of it all.

Because this is addressed to them, I use the second-person "you," as though no one else could be listening.

The Epilogue is written exclusively for and to them.

As anyone reads this, he should be struck with an impression that tells him that I want to be real. I have no campaign that needs supporters, no political agenda that requires my giving my words some special twist to their meaning, and I have no interest in hiding behind some badge of honor that suggests I am above and beyond mistakes. I am not. But what I want to do is to be sincerely honest in an effort to apologize for what I maintain is centuries of religious confusion. I sense—and perhaps it is psychological, not so much to help me sleep nights, but to help anyone who has been disillusioned by religion to have a chance to take another clear look—I have a need to talk. I have a need to apologize, and I have a need to explain.

I do this in dialog with my own sons in hope for the next generation, our children, who might easily be forgotten otherwise. They have, I maintain, a Biblical right to the truth. I can agree with our second President, John Adams, who once advised, "Children must not be wholly forgotten in the midst of public duties."

I start at the beginning.

Table of Contents

PART ONE
Living in Pennsylvania

1968	Married June 22
1969	Birth of Tim
	Purchased Chevelle
1971	Moved to Western Pennsylvania
	Zelienople for three weeks
	Moved to Freeport Road
1972	March, Visited Buffalo for three weeks
	Returned to Butler PA, lived in a motel for three weeks
	April, moved to Lyndora
	June, moved to Purvis Road
	Moved to West Street in Butler that Autumn
	Purchase Maverick
1973	Birth of James
1974	Purchased Chevy Nova
1975	Moved to McCandless Drive
	Moved to Canonsburg, PA that Autumn
1976	Moved to Burgettstown, PA
	Purchased Malibu Wagon
1979	Purchased Tercel
1983	Birth of Joshua
	Move to Sharpsville, PA
1984	Purchased burgundy Chevy

Once upon a Time

"Thou art one forever; and I
No dreamer, but Thy dream."
- C.S.Lewis

It was the summer of 1960. I was fifteen and very much a fifteen year old when it came to school and girls, but with a marked disability. I had asthma. Consequently I spent most of my time in quiet activity, watching TV, sitting at the kitchen table in conversation with family, or just day-dreaming about girls. But this summer was different, since the church paid my way to the Assembly of God religious camp at Troutsburg, NY on Lake Ontario, called Lakeview. I mention this, because there I had an interesting experience that I have been unable to forget.

It was Friday evening, the end of a week of mostly fun and games, some camping and nightly camp meetings, where all us teens gathered to sing and hear someone preach. I didn't find it boring. Quite the opposite, since I observed teens (kind-of) getting their lives all together as much as one week can begin to provide. It seemed real to me and somewhat exciting. After the main service that Friday, we gathered around a large bonfire and were given opportunity to tell everyone there what that week meant to us, since we were heading home Saturday morning.

I thought through, carefully, what I wanted to say. That's a good habit to get into. I approached the microphone when it was my turn and opened my mouth to give my prepared speech, when to my surprise— and I mean I was more surprised than anyone that I said it—I blurted out into the microphone, and I quote, "God is calling me into the ministry." Then I sat down on the grass in shock.

That was not at all what I intended to say! The thought of being a minister never had crossed my mind! You might wonder, where did it come from? Your guess is as good as mine. All I knew is that I couldn't get it out of my head. In some way, I can relate to C.S. Lewis:

They tell me, Lord, that when I seem
To be in speech with You,
Since You make no replies, it's all a dream
--One talker aping two.

And so it is, but not as they
Falsely believe, For I

3

Seek in myself the things I meant to say,
And lo! the wells are dry.

Then, seeing me empty, You forsake
The listener's part, and through
My dumb limps [lips?] breathe and into utterance wake
The thoughts I never knew.

Therefore You neither need reply
Nor can; for while we seem
Two walking. Thou art one forever; and I
No dreamer, but Thy dream -- April 1934

The following year, I missed camp, because I had a girlfriend I didn't want to leave, not even for one week. Missing her was too much to ask a 16-year-old, I guess.

There still was a lingering interest in ministry, even though it was eclipsed for the most part by other day-to-day interests. The sun was behind the clouds, so to speak, except for a ray or two from time to time, which pierced through all the mental meandering that a teenager is prone to. I mostly thought about girls, granted, but I did enjoy some church related things. I became a Sunday School teacher after turning 18. There was nothing in all of this that directly suggested ministry or pastoring. But there was one occasion which should have been a clear indicator that I was destined for Bible College.

My ex-girlfriend's brother, Gary Johnson, gave me a New Testament in Modern Greek. I spent a day at the Buffalo Public Library trying to translate just one word. This was in 1963, and with all that has happened in the last 45 years, I have not lost my interest in the Greek New Testament. If I could live my life over, I think the only thing I would change would be to get into a career that focused on it and the Classical Hebrew of the Old Testament. I continue to be warmly drawn to both.

I then attended the State University of New York for two years (1963-65) giving no thought to Bible school or ministry, until one day returning from school with me on the city bus a classmate reminded me that I had publicly announced my intention to go into the ministry. I must have said it in high school, probably after the 1960 camp experience. I don't remember, but I do remember what they said of me in the high school year book, and again I quote, "No man was ever great except by divine inspiration."

4

I flunked out of SUNY. That's a story, full of complaints, which has no relevance here, so I'll skip it.

It was August, 1965, and I had no future plans when my Sunday school teacher, Brother Wilson, who was locally employed as a chemist, not aware of what had happened between the State University and me, felt a need to warn me that he, too, once sensed a calling or passion for ministry, but stayed with the chemistry instead, and he had since regretted the choice. He exhorted me not to make the same mistake. So, with my own pastor's advice, I filled out an application for admission to Northeast Bible Institute (NBI), of the Assemblies of God, and with just weeks before the fall semester would begin, I was accepted. The pastor's wife consented to "get me there," and so, after a final meal—that sounds somewhat inappropriate, but that is what it was called—at Trotter's restaurant in Quakertown, PA, I was dropped off at the end of a long lane that wound its way from the main road, Route 18, up to the main campus.

I was alone and felt so, big time. They call it nostalgia. My dreams of the previous 20 years began recurring. These were day and night dreams which collected fond memories of my childhood, growing up in the city. They suggested to me that Providence was up to something. At least I wanted to believe that. Some of the day dreams added some sort of support to my contention that somehow there was a God that wanted me to do something or be someone that was somehow important to Him.

My mind went back. I remember at a very young age—perhaps, around 5 or 6—sitting on the porch with my cousin Dot, writing from the Bible some portion of, maybe, Ezekiel. I seem to recall an 'E' and 'z,' but that's all. The point is and was that it was the Bible, and my fascination with that book has not diminished.

Then there was asthma. Perhaps it's unimportant or, yes, easily explained other ways, but after very serious asthma attacks—my mom said I would be days in recovery—I would awaken in the middle of the day with a deep sense of peace. Was it medication or God? You judge. I think it was God. I would fall to sleep with full concentration only on breathing. I needed to focus on my next breath and the next, watching my chest rise with great labor and then fall until I would awake recovered. Back then, there was no medication given me for asthma except a chest caked with Vicks VapoRub and covered with heated cloth diapers. When I awoke from the nightmare of an asthma attack, I felt rested, and I could breathe again. I felt God.

Anyway, I would only return to Buffalo on visits.

Because God Made Thee Mine

Because, you come to me,
With naught save love,
And hold my hand and lift mine eyes above,
A wider world of hope and joy i see,
Because you come to me!
...
Because God made thee mine,
I'll cherish thee,
Through light and darkness, through all time to be,
And pray his love may make our love divine,
Because God made thee mine!
-- Guy D'Hardelot

Because was composed in 1902 by Guy D'Hardelot with lyrics by Edward Teschemacher. In 1913, it was a big hit for Enrico Caruso on the Victor label. And in 1948, Perry Como recorded it on RCA Victor. It became another million seller in his already successful career. Mario Lanza also recorded it for RCA Victor and it was popular during the summer of 1951. The song has also been recorded by Jerry Vale, Keely Smith, Placido Domingo, Sarah Vaughan, Frankie Laine, Nelson Eddy and many others recorded the song over the years. So to say the least, it is a standard.

The singular occasion of interest here is the fact that I sang it to your mother at our wedding. The last line stands out, "Because God made thee mine!" Over the years my belief in that possibility gave me cause for reflection every time we would argue or fight, verbally. And we fought! Sometimes you need an anchor to keep your tossing ship of marriage from hitting the rocks that would separate it into kindling. Know what I mean?

I want to talk about your mother and how we came to where we are. The route was sometimes circuitous, the long way round, where a little more dialog and understanding might have made the way to her arms straighter and faster. But it was during these times of emotional separation that I had opportunity to rehearse in my mind numerous details that kept bringing me back to the conclusion that God put us together.

And you thought all was forty plus years of total bliss?

Before I go there, you need to know the other so-called coincidences that pointed me toward your mom. I had told everyone for years, actually since I was 15 or so, that I would marry someone with brown eyes. I said it so often I came to believe it. Truth be told, I had my eyes on a certain brown eyed beauty as a teenager that I enjoyed being with. I came to doubt there was any chance for me, my self-opinion being so low, that in 1965 I gave up hoping and cut the emotional cord that bound my thoughts to her. I was free to love again.

But whom? I dated a blue-eyed girl during my first year at Bible school. Her name was Patricia, but Patricia said no to my proposal of marriage. (Smart girl.)

I went into survival mode, keeping my emotional distance from girls except as friends, and I had a few of them. They were like sisters to me—really—and I enjoyed talking to them, even holding hands. But I could not get serious for a couple reasons. Not only did I fear warming up to a young lady who had reason to keep her distance, but I also continued to have such a low self-esteem that I was convinced no woman would have me.

I was deceiving myself on a few counts. I also thought I was heavy even though I weighed in at only 145 pounds!

It isn't good to evaluate yourself, especially when your view of yourself is clearly skewed by environment, false pride, or some experience that doesn't do justice to depicting your real strengths, abilities, or potentials.

I flunked me on many subjects, and it wasn't until my third year at NBI that I began, just began, to take a reality check. I finally came to realize that as far as girls were concerned, it was really up to them whether or not they liked me. I would be as real as I could. I would be me and let them judge. And that's where your mother came into the picture.

Your mother was everywhere. She showed up at off-campus assignments. She was the freshmen class editor of our year book, while I was the assistant editor and organizing the entire project. We worked closely together on it. She would substitute for missing kitchen staff, working next to me while I scrubbed pots and pans between meals. And there was the occasional late night, when she would come in from her own off-campus job to eat a late meal, and I was still there working.

I kept running into her everywhere, until finally I decided to ask her to the Thanksgiving meal at school, a big event where we were waited on (didn't wait on others), all dressed up looking formal and important. At first she was reluctant to say yes, because campus rumor had me dating someone else. I came to regret the "sister" thing. But she finally did say yes. The reason why will have to be part of her memoirs.

Regarding the dinner, I liked it!. I don't mean the food, I mean the date! I probably enjoyed the food, too, whatever we had. It was probably turkey. Who cared?

I began to work with mom, not only on an intellectual level but also an emotional one. I still kept a little distance just in case she began throwing hints that this was just a weak friendship. She never did send such vibes. Instead, she wondered what I was really up to. Fish or cut bait, John, was how I read her sentiment. I decided to go fishing.

That Spring, I asked her to marry me and she said yes. It was then that I looked at her eyes and noticed that they were brown.

Coincidence? Unconscious decision? Or God?

I choose God. I say this because I had come to hope that somehow, even in an unseen way, He would be leading me, making decisions for me if need be. This might make crazy or even errant theology, but it was mine. I hoped that all the coincidences put together somehow outweighed mere chance and that it had to be God.

I asked her to marry me four months hence. I had feared I would lose her, since she was not planning to return the next semester. Right or wrong, we set the date for June.

Here is the skinny. I had no real job. I was working on campus for a buck an hour for maybe three hours a day, and I had a school bill. I had no car. She did, but I had no license to drive. There was no apartment to rent. Apparently the students with forethought and planning had rented them all already. That was all right. I guess. Because I also had no furniture.

Another interesting coincidence occurred when I needed a job, but being out in the country with no connections, I couldn't see any way to find one. So I walked the lane and talked. Talked to myself? Talked to the trees? Talked to God? I think C, because my main prayer was simple passion and a little anxiety. I told God that if He required it, I would go door to door—I guess that meant farmhouse to farmhouse—and beg people to hire me. One dollar an hour, 70 dollars a month, wouldn't cut it!

This happened on a Thursday evening. The following day—I kid you not—the editor-in-chief of our yearbook, whom I allegedly worked with although I didn't know what he did, approached me, representing the management of the Longacre Family Poultry Company in Franconia. He offered me a job starting at $2.25 an hour. This was the highest paying job for students in the area. I could start Friday morning.

I asked if I could start Monday instead. Such audacity on my part must have brought a smile to God's face if anything would. And just as a point of information, a year later, new management at Longacre's made it impossible to get a job so easily there. It would take forms and interviews after this.

Would you like an interesting footnote? Tim was born 12 months into our marriage and less than nine months since I took out medical insurance at Longacre's, which meant that the insurance policy I had at work wouldn't kick in yet to pay hospital expenses. Mr. Longacre himself, the owner of the plant, went to bat for us, and the next thing we knew, the insurance did pay the entire medical expense.

Here is the biggest coincidence yet. In our search for an apartment, we visited the local real estate agent in Greenlane. It was a small town with only one agency, and they told us nothing was available. I had figured other students had been there ahead of us, a fact confirmed by the readiness by which the agent responded to my quest, and I figured if any thing had been available, it was taken. Our search turned up nothing until I visited a friend, Frank Leone, whom I met at my new off-campus job. He disagreed with the agent, since just a day before, he had been apartment-hunting, and they had showed him a one-bedroom, third-story apartment that was available but too small for his family of four.

So we went back to the agency and related our confusion over our friend's story. It was then that the agent remembered that he did have a small one bedroom apartment in Greenlane which he had forgotten about. It was ours if we wanted it, for fifty dollars per month, utilities included. It was perfect, perfectly located, and the price was within budget. How many students came and went through that agency looking for something, students who were turned away, disappointed?

We were married that June, the 22nd (let's see... yes, the 22nd), and in our own apartment, furniture and all, only one mile from campus.

Oh yes, I got my license to drive, thanks to your mother's persistence.

B'reshit

I will make the darkness light before you

B'reshit is Hebrew for "in the beginning," and this is the story of our B'reshit. I met your mother, and about eight months later we were married. The ellipsis of November through June, our engagement period, I wish to hop and skip over, to bring you to our true beginning. The thing I remember about this time was trying desperately to get alone with your mom to kiss her. This was next to impossible, since we were at a Bible school that enforced a six-inch rule. Two people in love had to be six inches apart at all times, and that meant no holding hands. I didn't like the six-inch rule. Once, in revolt, I pulled Mom into the office of the Dean of Women, the Chief of the Romance Police, and before the Dean returned, I kissed Mom. A laughable memory, but a bold one nevertheless.

Mom did not attend the second semester from January to May, but she did drive the 80 miles every other Saturday to see me. My heart leaped to see her, and then I would try to find a hiding place to smooch. One time, we tried the park, but the park warden made us move on.

I was 24, and Mom, 26. Can anyone remember back that far? Our first year as a couple, our first fight, our first ministry, our first child, my first car (actually, Mom's), and undoubtedly a hundred other firsts for both of us, since we were miles from family in a small town with few friends and little to do but work and retire for the night into our two-room apartment on the third floor.

One might consider this ideal, since there were no in-laws to tell us what to do or how to behave. But this formula only works well if you have some idea of what to do, which, it turned out, we didn't. We were two strangers that met just six months earlier in a school environment that encouraged distance when it came to romance, and now we were living together, whatever that was suppose to imply. To make matters worse, no one ever taught me a reasonable definition for romance. I learned duty and responsibility, so I went to work for eight hours and school for six and slept the rest of the time each day, leaving my bride to find something to read or do on her own.

For a brief time, at Longacre, mom worked where I worked. It was the only time in forty years of marriage that we worked together. We stacked and packed chicken rolls.

How romantic!

11

Actually, for me, it was romantic, until the night foreman saw fit to break us up. He rehired a young college kid who took my place on the line, while I went off to scrub large pots. When I was in the neighborhood, I would glance over at mom innocently laughing and conversing with this newcomer and inevitably, my jealousy got the better of me. I made her quit the job. I can't remember what logic I used to convince her that it was for the better for her to spend 24 hours a day in a two-room apartment with nothing to do.

She needed a TV to watch! So we drove to Sears in Reading and bought a small, 11-inch, black-and-white TV set.

Yeah, that spells romance.

September, 1968, three months into our marriage, we decided it would be appropriate to have a child. This would give my young bride something to do. Truth be told, the timing was ideal. I wanted a son.

In retrospect, I did little planning. Most of my life, I must admit, was regulated by the demand of the moment. Whether I was managing crises or just waiting around for some opportunity, I had a laid-back approach to life that suggested that providence was in charge of things, or maybe that no one was. I didn't realize this at the time, because there always seemed so little to decide. But life turned routine when daily responsibilities included eight hours work and six hours school. Only the weekends provided some free time, and then Mom and I typically made the 80-mile trip to Vineland to see your Grandma and Grandpa. If we went to Quakertown, to the Q-Mart, or anyplace else, it was what I thought Mom wanted. I took very little initiative to surprise her.

How am I doing as a husband? I guess it's time I shared with you a rather strange experience I had in that first year. Mom and I were attending a church service locally in Greenlane, and it happened during the song service. I cannot remember the song we were singing at the time, but I do remember a strange, what I would call, "anxiety" rolled over me, starting at my head and working its way down my body toward my feet. I can remember—I kid not—getting a terrible case of the shakes, not because I felt cold. I didn't.

I simply began to shake uncontrollably. It had never happened before and hasn't happened since. Make a note of this if it seems important for your diagnoses.

I became distracted. I still knew where I was, but I didn't want to be there, and whatever others were doing or singing, count me out. I was not only losing it, as they say, but this was a unique experience that had no apparent connection with my reality, my past experiences, my upbringing, or my hopes for the future. My mind was blank. I could connect no thought with the shakes, no worry, no ongoing anxiety. Is this what happens to newlyweds? I had no idea.

Almost completely overcome by the feeling and next to panic as to what to do about it, I grabbed the song book as a distraction hoping that if I just begin to read hymns, read anything at hand, it might politely pass. I opened the hymn book to song 154 and began to read the chorus:

I will make the darkness light before you,
What is wrong I'll make it right before you,
All the battles I will fight down for you,
And the high place I'll bring down.

As I read it, the nervousness began to leave my body. A peaceful calm began to work its way up my body until I was completely at ease, as if on darvoset or percocet or something. I was calm, completely relaxed and thinking it had passed for good, not caring to analyze the experience but simply to forget that it ever happened. I looked over at my young wife to see what song we were on and began to thumb my way to that place in my hymn book.

I do not exaggerate when I tell you what happened next, what I figure you can anticipate. The shakes returned a second time, starting at my head and working their way to my legs. You would think that at this moment, I would have frantically fingered through the hymnal for song 154, but I didn't. I didn't have to. I simply closed and reopened the hymnal. It opened at, yes, song 154. I began again to read the words of the song and its chorus, while the anxiety again began to dissipate from toe to head as before.

Now, what do you make of that? I was never diagnosed with mental illness; neither had anyone to my knowledge in my family. And I pride myself in being first in line when it comes to seeking a clear and concise scientific explanation. My problem is that by science, I mean proof, not just theory. I never did see medicine or modern scientific inquiry as a threat to faith. It is just the opposite. When science draws a blank, we have a right now to think God. If later science comes up with a proof, God will not take offense if we take it back from Him. My experience has shown me that much of life will never need to be taken back.

I then did what I had previously. I found my place in the current song and began to sing, when the shakes returned for a third time.

You think I am making this up? I wish I were. But fiction is not my thing. You think I really didn't have a singular anxiety attack? If you know me, you know that anxiety was one of my middle names, so this had to be of the ordinary variety. But it wasn't. I can't explain it and I am struggling to describe it.

Even after forty years, I can remember what I felt. I tend to forget words and thoughts, maybe faces, but not feelings. I guess there is a difference between crazy and just plain weird. So be it, but let me tell you what I didn't feel. I wasn't lightheaded. I wasn't cold, as I mentioned. I wasn't dizzy. My eyesight was not blurring or broken with spots. I was not in physical pain, and I was not angry or feeling depressed.

Understandably, I was concerned, maybe a bit frightened.

Did I eat a good breakfast that morning? Can't remember. I know what low blood sugar feels like, and this was not it.

This time when the nervousness came back, I choose to grab the Bible instead of the song book. I opened it at random as I had with the hymnal. My interest was in finding a distraction, something to get my mind off this craziness and something that could calm me. The Bible held special meaning to me, so it was a likely candidate for the task. I opened to Isaiah 43 and began to read:

> But now thus saith the LORD that created thee, O Jacob, and he that formed thee, O Israel, Fear not: for I have redeemed thee, I have called [thee] by thy name; thou [art] mine.

As I read down to verse 19 I became enveloped in a peace that never left.

> Remember ye not the former things, neither consider the things of old. Behold, I will do a new thing; now it shall spring forth; shall ye not know it? I will even make a way in the wilderness, [and] rivers in the desert.

The anxiety, the shakes, the nervousness was gone. I stood there in some disbelief, not because I had interpreted the scripture in any personal way, but because I wasn't so sure the nervousness wouldn't return. I kept the Bible open to the text before me and read it again and again, building a confidence that I was free from this strange experience.

I was free. The shakes were over and done. I returned to the song service and joined in with the congregation as if nothing had happened.

It was over, but what did it mean? How was I to interpret this? I reflected back on it in our second year and came up with some explanations.

Hermeneutics is the study of interpreting the Bible. It is the science of using grammar and certain techniques to extract the meaning behind the scriptures. We try to be careful interpreting the Bible, because it is so easy, as with statistics, to get the Bible to say almost anything someone wants it to say. We use sound grammar, based on good Greek or Classical Hebrew. Generally, too, we take literally that which is meant literally, and stay away from symbolizing something that can take a literal meaning without carrying literalness to absurdity. It is also possible for a prophecy to have a double meaning both historically in reference to Israel and in reference to Christ. It is also possible for a verse to have personal meaning, provided that meaning does not conflict with its historical or theological one.

Here is where my mind starts reflecting on these verses in Isaiah. The former things could be my single life, and the new thing springing forth could be going from single to married with a child and a church inside one year.

I think so. I took comfort in thinking that somehow God wanted me to know that I was on a good course. Things weren't going haywire. My life was not out of control.

Our first year together had first-step challenges that—sorry, Son— gave me cause for reflection at the time and a slight feeling of possible regret that I had blown it. Whatever "it" was, being married, working in the church, going to school, I was perhaps not the man for the job.

I was full-time at school plus working all night scrubbing pots. I was neglecting my bride, and now I was soon to graduate with a new baby and no clear direction as to what to do next.

I was trying to play youth leader at the church of mom's teen years in Vineland, NJ. The pastor at the time, Rev. Harry Snook, who also officiated at our wedding, called Mom his "right arm" and asked her to organize some youth work in the church. That meant me, too, but I really hated the job. Taking kids to skating rinks was not my interest. I wanted to explore Scripture, maybe even do some archaeological stuff. Some student caught the idea for me in our 1969 yearbook. He wrote of me, "Professor of Greek, Hebrew, and Kweedersway." Kwedersway must mean computer programming, since back then they would not have had a better word to foretell my involvement with information technology.

We met with Rev. Snook, who coincidentally was also the Home Mission's Director for the New Jersey District of the Assemblies of God. He invited me to candidate the A of G church in West Cape May, NJ. Thinking that the way to go was pastoring, we left for West Cape May that August, 1969, with our 2-month-old son and hoped for a new beginning.

Shell Beach

Today is a smooth white seashell, hold it close
and listen to the beauty of the hours.
--Unknown

Shell beach doesn't exist any longer. The authorities must have cleaned it up for the tourists, but back in 1969 it was my favorite hide-a-way. It was a portion of the Cape May coastline that was separated from the main beach by a wall of rocks, and as the sea is in the habit of doing, it deposited all kinds of seashells on this stretch of sand about 100 yards long for someone like me to find. When I needed a peace-break from our first church, I would go there to search through the ruins for shells of singular interest.

It was an artist's world of sight and sound, or if you were a marine pathologist, a kind of seaside Bones, you would enjoy this graveyard of limitless sea stories.

I just wanted to be there among the shells, some crunching underfoot, others rescued as keepsakes for my mantel. And the air and the sea and the waves and the sun were positively addictive. I never felt more at peace than when I was there rummaging about among the treasures of God's primeval world.

In our second year at West Cape May, on a regular visit to one of the men in the church, at a gas station in Wildwood where he worked, I asked him to tell me about this amusement park everyone was talking about. I had never seen it. He pointed in an easterly direction and said, "Walk one block that way." I did and wow! Everything from Ferris wheels to roller coasters, places to eat, souvenir shops, you name it, and I had had no idea it was there.

But I knew about shell beach. That must say something about me, though I don't know what.. Am I a workaholic? I prefer shells to bumper cars? I like cheaper amusements, like free shells?

Jump ahead to 1983. We were in Florida on a business trip, just outside Orlando, with all three of you boys, and I didn't show you Disney World.

In our first ministry, we were 10 miles out to sea, as they used to say, because one had to cross a bridge to get there. We lived on Broadway, exactly one mile down from the Atlantic Ocean. I have fond memories of watching Mom and you,Tim, taking off for the beach, You wearing your bathing suit. The fact that I was too busy to join you says something about the lack of fun that characterized my approach to life in those days.

We went to West Cap May on a mission. There was a little church on Broadway which was formally maintained by a dwindling group of parishioners, who found it increasingly harder and harder to manage. So they arranged for the Assemblies of God to take it over, in order to keep the church open. The former pastor, Pastor Eckstein, had been there eleven years and now sought to move on, but the arrangement had been made in writing that if we kept the church going for seventeen years—I don't know why seventeen—the church would become the property of the Assemblies of God. Someone needed to be found to fill the pulpit for just six more years.

We took care of two of those years. Today there is in Cold Springs an Assembly of God church which was built initially off the sale of the old building that we pastored. And the little church on Broadway? Today it is a restaurant, believe it or not.

Of all the places we have been in our travels, this is the one place I would like to return to for a final hooray.

I don't want a second chance to make a success of things, because I don't think we were unsuccessful. Success is one of those words you can define whatever way you want. For me, our first church was a success, because statistically we survived it and left the then-congregation with a building that had equity worth something for a future investment. Granted, we ran out of money, and the church could not afford to keep paying us the fifty dollars a week for living. Granted, the church didn't grow under our ministry, and I think I did make a few enemies. *Enemies* is too strong a term. I must have disillusioned a few people who left us. But I liked the town and the ocean air.

But our first two weeks there could have been an omen. They rented out our living quarters, the parsonage, for 125 dollars a week—or was it a day?—while we spent the time living in the Westerlands' garage. The Westerlands were an elderly couple who attended briefly. They moved away soon afterward.

For those first two weeks we ate Jersey tomatoes and tried to stay warm in our one-room, makeshift apartment, which the Westerlands furnished with (I think) antiques.

West Cape May, perhaps because it was our first church, generated a lot of anxiety in a young minister who, truth be told, didn't know what he was doing. On one visit to Vineland to enjoy some R & R and grandma Miller's cooking—we made this trip every Monday for two years—

18

we stopped in to see Pastor Snook. I asked him pointedly what I should be doing to grow the little church in West Cape May. Back then, success was defined by the number of people in attendance, and I wasn't being so successful—in those terms—since we had only about twenty people attending on a given Sunday. During the summer, attendance was up by a half-dozen visitors, and once in a while, someone from the Coast Guard base would show up to check us out.

Pastor Snook advised me to visit people on a regular basis: new people, people who were already attending, anyone I could, to make a public statement that ours was a church that loved and cared about the community. I don't know if his advice went to my heart as much as it went to my head. I made a visit to Wildwood one afternoon, with Mom and Tim joining me for the ride. Mom elected to wait in the car while I popped in and out for a quick visit. I returned to the car three hours later. I had left my family for three hours, while I was shooting the breeze with a family who was probably wondering if I was planning to stay for dinner and spend the night. I was visiting people for visitation's sake and hadn't discovered the art of balancing the visit with other responsibilities and interests. It would be years before my personality would get the hang of it.

Is this event significant? Probably, because it is revealing. There was and is something about me that makes pastoring, which I love doing, nonetheless a challenge. It may not be a productive exercise, but I am trying to step back and view the life I lived through memory's eye and understand what it was about me that made me do what I did.

Another good thing for me to have learned about myself is that I was incredibly naive. I didn't always know what was plainly in front of me. I trusted people implicitly, simply because they claimed to be Christian. I wasn't streetwise.

Joan was fifteen when we arrived, and during our first week there, she disappeared, seemingly ran away. It turned out that her boyfriend at the time was AWOL from the army, and she was with him in the City of Love, that is, in Philadelphia. The military finally caught up with him and took him back to Fort Dix. The situation was delicate, because her parents didn't want him with their daughter. The details of the story are not important for this narrative, because I have nothing good or ill to say about the players in this account, except myself. I made a trip to Fort Dix to arrange for the boyfriend one last meeting with Joan, hoping that it meant goodbye, because I favored the parents' wishes in the matter.

What pastor travels upstate and spends the day to arrange for a reunion between a teenager and her boyfriend, who incidentally was rumored to have been already married. My purpose was to move slowly, hoping she would not become defensive and that she would see the better part of wisdom in this situation. Fortunately, the two did break up, and Joan remained at home and in the church. But this trip was a hint of things to come. It already indicated that I was quick to get involved, even if I was in over my head.

Just looking at me, one could observe my naiveté. Joan always sat next to me when I picked her family up for church each Sunday. I am inclined to think in retrospect that this was classic transference. Whether that made me a dad, brother, or boyfriend I can't say, but your Mom caught it and put me on the alert. Nothing came of it, and perhaps there was nothing there anyway, but being streetwise and understanding women were new topics to me, topics about which I would not learn so quickly.

The pastorate is more than sermons and prayers. It is also relationships, and pastors need to wisely define these relationships. I was only beginning to see this.

I was already showing signs of getting overly involved with people I was supposed to care about. I would pick up a carload of people in Wildwood for church, seven miles each way, which meant four round trips each week. We had two services on Sunday. We made that trip for two years until our car tires were literally bald and the springs were gone. The floor in the front seat was rusted through from the salt air, exposing the road beneath. That old car also made a trip to Fort Lee, Virginia, for Jim, a member of the church who would otherwise have been considered AWOL. Jim had missed his bus ride. When will I learn my limits? At least Mom and I were able to make a weekend getaway out of it, visiting the Capital.

The big story in this first church was Luke. It was in West Cape May where we met Luke, a professional house painter who moved down the coast from Trenton to find work with all the new development going up along the South Jersey shore. Luke wanted a partner. He was tired of hiring people and trying to work out with the government all the details which a small business is required to work out. When you hire, you have to consider payroll tax withholdings and various insurances, all of which costs big bucks.

So, I became his partner, which legally is a simpler business relationship, at least on paper. He knew we needed the money, and since he attended church, albeit on a hit-and-miss basis, he asked me to join him. I was a professional painter with my own business. It went to my head.

20

Things were fine for awhile. I made three dollars an hour, Luke made six, and God made one. What this actually meant was that the net profit was split three ways 6:3:1 among Luke, me, and the church. Luke actually had God drawn into the partnership agreement as a legal partner for one dollar an hour, or a tithe. We used the dollar an hour money to remodel the church during the winter of 1970-71, which raised the value of the property by an estimated 5,000 dollars. This was good money back then. And these were good times, too. We bought about 370-dollars worth of supplies from a local lumber yard and changed the building's ceiling from looking like an assembly hall to looking like a miniature cathedral, in my eyes, with a ridge board, pillars, and caps around the sanctuary. It was made of grade-one pine, walnut-stained. The ridge board came in three parts, representing the Trinity. There were thirteen rafters, one of them cut short up against the nursery. These represented the apostles and Judas Iscariot, who had also been cut off. There were seven pillars, seven being the number of perfection.

We were having fun, but it would end, thanks in part to Santa Claus. Santa Claus was an elderly man for whom we contracted to paint the outside of his house in Cape May. We called him Santa because of his full-length, white beard and pot belly. Well, Santa was unhappy with the completeness of our work. What we had done he was pleased with, but he contended that we should have also done A, B, and C.

We had in the meantime moved on to our next contract, restoring the old Chalfonte Hotel in Cape May. (Google it!) We painted it, sixty plus rooms, including the side house and dining rooms.

Luke felt that we should try to please the elderly gentleman. Maybe it was good for business, but when I calculated it in, my 3 dollars an hour had become $1.37. I said no, and since I was a named partner, I felt I had the right to stand my ground on the subject. Luke disappeared for a few days from the Chalfonte while I worked without him. Luke's oldest son also was working on the project, working the spray gun. Luke returned after satisfying the gentleman, but things would never be the same between us after that. We kept getting on each other's nerves. He would decide to do something, and I would feel I had the right to disagree. Remember, after all, I was a partner. We never finished the Chalfonte together. I had resigned the church and moved on before we completed the job.

My pride was more important to me at the time than my friendship with Luke. I cannot imagine myself thinking that way today, but at the time, Luke was not going to make decisions for me. I was a partner and had a vote, too. Looking back, I think this was for me an esteem issue, but back then the cause was far from clear. I just felt the way I felt and acted on it, until our partnership was strained and our friendship needed to be revisited.

I received a phone call from Frank Leon. He and his family had moved back to Aliquippa, when he learned that a small Bible school had started where he might obtain the education he sought. That's his story, but ours takes up with a phone call in which he put us in touch with one of the faculty members at the school, Brother Bill Bailey. Brother Bailey gave me hope of a position at the little school of about a couple dozen students. They needed a Greek teacher.

I'm there! What did I know? Did someone say, "Think before you jump?" August of 1971, Mom and I quit the church and moved to Western Pennsylvania.

A few years later we revisited Cape May, then with two sons. Jim, you were about three, so this would have been in 1976. We met with Luke, and he asked us to come back to Cape May and rejoin the team. For reasons then obvious, we couldn't. But it was nice to reconcile.

We would revisit the Cape a few more times after, but Luke had moved on. And as for the art of reconciliation, I had more lessons coming, in our future adventures with people.

Then and even now, there was and is something drawing about Southern New Jersey. Even the salt air was good for me. I didn't make a big deal out of it, but while there in 1970, I developed what the doctor thought might be pleurisy. X-rays showed nothing, however. Nothing! That was odd, since I grew up with asthma and had had pneumonia, double and single, with and without bronchitis, a number of times as a youth. Now my lungs were clear? They had never been clear. Every summer in Buffalo from age 18 to 22, I had to have a TB test to confirm that the cloudiness in the X-rays of my lungs was not because of tuberculosis. The doctor in Cape May was a bit put out with me when he told me one final time that there was "nothing wrong with your lungs."

There was always something intoxicating about Southern New Jersey for me. It was a hideaway. In my daydreams it seems to be a perfect place to find a small group of people that wouldn't mind studying the Bible with me.

In this small resort town, I had begun to learn big lessons about relationships. But the big lessons about forgiveness and mercy and reconciliation and, yes, romance were still to come.

It's a Wonderful Life

…thinking you are bullet-proof.
You're so hyped up and pumped so much,
you can't wait to rush in and attack.
--Urban Dictionary

I did a bad thing. I wasn't on drugs, but I was on Biblical Greek. Let me teach it anywhere at anytime for any amount, and I am there! This has proven over the years to be a realistic appraisal of my stupidity. Teaching Greek isn't bad, but running here and there to do it isn't smart. The worse part was that in 1971, I didn't think to invite my spouse into my dreams. When I thought she had no interest in joining me, I pretended she had only to be told about my vision. I was prepared to go alone.

And I did; I left for Western Pennsylvania Bible Institute (WPBI) in Butler, PA, informing her that I would be back to get her and little Timmy. Of course, I would return. Of course, I had no intention of leaving them in New Jersey, but this would be an exercise in dragging rather than in persuading, and the thought of making it a joint adventure, regrettably, never crossed my mind.

As far as your mother goes, she didn't seem as gung-ho as I. To be gung-ho, according to one contributor to Urban Dictionary, means "to be so psyched out for war… thinking you are bullet-proof. You're so hyped up and pumped so much, you can't wait to rush in and attack…"

That about sums it up. I was off to Western PA without so much as a goodbye kiss. It was early in the morning when I drove away, leaving your mother sleeping. She probably wasn't.

Pennsylvania is basically a tale of two towns, Lyndora and Butler, even though we spent the first two weeks in Zelienople. There are some fond memories for me here and also some things hard to talk about. But all in all, I am totally reconciled with everything that happened, even though it might have been wiser on reflection not to have gone to Western PA when and how we did. Yet I don't know this for sure.

Now, maybe I need to say something here that you should recall every time I call myself stupid. This is a confession, not one more occasion to beat myself up. We all have regrets over stupid things we've done, and some of those decisions have lasting effects, but this should never mean that life has descended into some lower level of reality from which we cannot crawl or climb out. I crawled out.

Perhaps an example of how stupid I was capable of being might help to evaluate this reflective moment. We were riding in our new car, a 1972 Ford Maverick, which was great on gas. I decided to see how far I could go on one tank. This was a little test meant to quench my curiosity only. No one needed to know. No one wanted to know, except me. We were driving on Interstate 79, heading south toward Butler, when I remembered to look at the gas gauge and noticed we had less than an eighth of a tank of gasoline left and probably about fifty miles till home. I don't know. I didn't treat this as a scientific study. What idiot does? I only know that I became anxious when the meter read no gas left and we still were not home. It was late at night. Gas stations were closed.

We lived on West Street in Butler, on a slight incline which was valleyed in front of the house we lived in. I was more relaxed when we reached the town, and I actually forgot all about the test as we neared home. The car began to stall, and I wondered why. I thought I had engine trouble. It was a Ford after all. (It did, in fact, turn out to be a lemon. A mechanic told me that he had discovered a 1969 Mercury part in our brand new Maverick. If so, this is unconscionable.)

The engine conked out on the hill above our home, and I put it in neutral and coasted to a stop in front of the house. It was then I remembered. We were out of gas.

I was out of gas in more ways then one. My career was in trouble because the school didn't want me full time. My health was in trouble. My blood pressure was up, and I needed eventually to go on part-time disability and a diet. My marriage was strained and probably would have been in trouble as well had there been recourse for Mom or I, because even though we loved each other, we felt alone. We were each other's only friend, it seemed, and that friendship wasn't working. We weren't talking. Yelling a little, but not talking.

And did I mention: There was little to no money. We went to Butler with $1,700 less moving expenses. This was my last pay from working on the Chalfonte in Cape May. I spent it before paying tax on it. I owed about 200 federal tax dollars.

Our first place of residence in Butler was on Freeport Road. When the money ran out, our rent of about 200 some dollars a month ran out. If one does the math, it isn't immediately obvious where the money had gone. We had been in the area about seven months, August through February, and most of it probably went into moving and first- and last-month's rent plus security deposit and regular living expenses. Our old Chevy from West Cape May days had no heater. It turned out, the rheostat in the system was not functioning, but we couldn't afford to fix it.

We lived there through February, 1972, when we had to move, with no place to go. I had taken a job working for a professional painter out of Sarver, but it wasn't steady work. In fact, during the winter months, we had only a couple small inside paint jobs. That was when we packed up our things and went to see Grandma King in Buffalo for a few weeks.

About three weeks later I brought mom and Tim back into Butler. I left Buffalo simply because I didn't want to be there. I didn't think that was where we were supposed to be living. I came to Butler to teach Greek, so I was determined to try again. We rolled into town in a car packed with blankets, towels, clothes, and some kitchen stuff, everything we owned. When we came down route 422, I had a terrible headache, no clue where to live, and no money. I drove through Butler and headed south on Route 8, when we saw a little rather run-down looking motel, a dozen or so apartments in a row, plain-looking on the outside, and on the inside one-room with a double bed, a TV set with rabbit ears that didn't work well, a shower, and a little kitchen area with a small stove and re-frigerator.

The manager of the motel would let us go week to week for the rent. We paid 25 dollars at the end of each week. I made a phone call to Sarver, my old boss and he, taking sympathy, lined up a couple inside paint jobs that paid the rent week after week until an apartment in Lyndora opened up for us. In natural terms, the only good thing was that spring was just around the corner.

I was too wrapped up in my own challenges to realize that I had left my young wife of 3 years and my two-year-old with nothing to do day after day, except maybe worry about what brilliant idea I would dream up next. No wonder at all that she didn't have that much to say to me. About all I had were mini-messages on faith and trust, and they might not have been working for me, but trust was what I was learning. I was-n't sure why we were in this situation. Did God have any real thing to do with it? Was this totally my own doing or undoing?

Regardless, our ship didn't sink. We took in some water, but I was too busy bailing to think of much else. Every phone call from McElheny, my boss, was one more phone call that gave us one more week's rent and groceries. Meanwhile, I was in communication with the school, and they promised us soon that a rent-free two rooms would open up at the school itself in Lyndora.

So we moved to Lyndora. We took two back rooms at the school, connected directly to two classrooms. Mom had to keep Tim quiet to avoid disturbing the students. Fun life! Going from kitchen to bedroom reading books, playing with toys, whatever, while waiting for classes to end so they could get out of this human cage.

When classes ended for the day, we could use the shower in the basement. The water source came from a pipe protruding five-plus feet off the ground from the wall. There was plenty of shivering while I, dripping wet, ran upstairs to get dressed.

One might say that the three weeks at the motel was in preparation for this step up. One might say so, if one wants to get slapped. There was no way to clean up the mess, unless it were to become clear to both of us that God was directing us, not just bailing us out of our self-made prison.

Honesty is good. Fake humility or fake praise, even toward God, benefits no one. I didn't want to tidy up what was turning into a real mess, but I also fault no one. The benefit of reflecting on the hard times is two-fold. Learn from it to avoid the stupid parts in the future, and learn to empathize with those who made the journey with you and may not have found it to be so wonderful. As I relate this, I am beginning not to like me. But my only mistake was jumping out of the frying pan. Who knew?

There had to be some good times, right? Yes, of course. We made some life-long friendships with the Thompsons and the Davises. Denny and Amy Thompson and Gary and Jan Davis were students, and they had their own problems – or "faith walk" as we called it. We learned to join them for a time to reflect on reality, to pray together, and just to laugh over a game of Trouble. Who chose that one, I wonder.

The best thing was learning to trust God. When someone now enters my life who is fearful that things are not going to work out favorably, they get no sympathy from me. Empathy, yes, because Mom and I were there. Sympathy, no, because it is impossible for me to think that God might ignore the plight of someone who is trusting in Him to do something. I kept thinking of Isaiah 43. Sorry for the mini-sermon, but when you've run the rapids, still water is a splash.

We lived in Lyndora only while we were waiting on a double-wide mobile home, which was going to be set up on Purvis Road in Butler. The mortgage would be a couple hundred dollars a month, and I just needed a thousand dollars up-front to pour the foundation pillars and dig a well and a leach bed for the septic system.

I didn't have a thousand dollars, so I asked Grandma King for it. She borrowed it for me. I never paid her back. This is why I believe in paying some things forward when the opportunity to repay no longer is there.

Things were looking up. We would be living in a brand new home. It smelled new. When the carpet guys were installing the living room wall-to-wall carpet, you, Tim, our three year old, walked up to me holding a razor blade which the carpet guy had used to cut the carpet in place. It seems a tiny thing now, perhaps, but you were not injured by something that in your then-little hand could have sliced you deeply. God watches?

To help with the mortgage, we took in a male boarder, a student from the school. So now, I was working as a painter, and I had about $70 a month coming in as a teacher at the School, which now moved to its new location on the other end of Purvis Road. We also had a boarder. Things were looking up.

Did I mention that I could be stupid?

I discovered on my body what was later diagnosed as a small, harmless mole. It still lives with me. But I made a doctor's appointment and failed to inform Mr. McElheny. The following day, I went into work, feeling better about the mole, only to be told that I had forfeited my job when I failed to call in sick. There would be no second chance. Now I was out of work, and that would make a huge difference in our income. We no longer could afford the mortgage. It was that straightforward. We could not live there.

To say that money was tight understated the fact. We were getting $91 worth of food stamps from a sweet, elderly caseworker who seemed to instinctively realize our situation, but when she was replaced with a younger woman, we were charged $41 for the $91 worth of stamps. We did not have $41, so that well went dry.

And the male boarder left.

The septic system wasn't working either, since the rain run-off was finding its way through a broken field tile into our leach system.

Tim, you got your hand caught in the brand new screen door, because one of the men from the church didn't see you there when he closed the door on your hand. The emergency room visit was $29, which we could not pay for months, and the hospital let us know with regularity that we still owed it.

I knew we may have to move. What else is new?

But first, I tried to get another job. So I filled out an application for employment as a custodian with the Butler Area School District, submitted it, and forgot about it. It sounds like true faith, submit and forget, but that is not how it worked. The school district had no positions available but would get back to me if one opened up.

Meanwhile, I applied with some outfit to sell Rainbow vacuum cleaners. Ever hear of the Rainbow vacuum cleaner? Me neither, and it didn't even symbolize any divine promise, it was simply a desperate attempt to stay afloat. A Methodist minister in Cold Spring, NJ (near Cape May) once said that every minister should first be a salesman, since he is selling the gospel message.

Whatever. I guess I am not good at evangelism, because night after night, I would have to come home and report to your mom what kind of money I hadn't earned. The big problem was that along with the vacuum cleaner, we had incentive gifts that we could give away to entice the customer to purchase the cleaner. The first gift was pure incentive. The second gift replaced our commission, and commission was all we worked for.

Yes, I did give away my commission, and yes, stupid, stupid, stupid, but I wanted to get the hang of selling the thing.

We surely were going to have to move.

From time to time, money would show up in the mailbox. Sometimes, it was from Grandma and Grandpa Miller. Sometimes, it was from an unknown source. But it put food on the table.

We bought a bag of cornmeal which was our canary in the mine. When it was gone, we would be, too. But we never were down to the cornmeal.

This entangled mesh I was finding impossible to untie. It reminded me of my first day in kindergarten. The teacher called for all of us to join her on the main carpet in the center of the main room, after we had put on our sneakers. New sneakers still have a memorable aroma to me. But I got a knot in my one sneaker I could not get out. For a four-year-old who now thinks he has done something unpardonable and will never get to see his mother again, this was a most traumatic moment. And here I was again with a knotted sneaker I could not untie.

I thought the school board at the Bible school was on my case over the unpaid utility bills, which they were aware of by opening our mail. I thought they considered me irresponsible, because that is basically what their messenger, Brother Bailey, for whom I continue to hold the greatest respect, related.

Brother Bailey had invited us to come to Western Pennsylvania and teach, and now he was dying of a recurrence of multiple-myeloma. He was a dear friend and neighbor. He was the perfect ambassador, since he could relate the board's interests, and they knew neither I nor Mom would jump at him. Brother Bailey sat with us at our little but new, round, dining room table that sat four, while he went down the list of bills unpaid and more than one month in arrears. The board saw me as behaving irresponsibly. Their biggest concern might have been the mortgage, which now I could not afford.

It was also during this time that we got a visit from the IRS. I looked out the window as a bright, red VW Bug pulled up at the end of our driveway. A middle-aged gentleman in a smart business suit started up the walk, when I called to Mom to ask her if she knew anyone who owned a Doodlebug. She didn't.

Answering the door, I was introduced to an IRS agent. They wanted their $200 from the Chalfonte, and they finally caught up with me after one year. Their agent sat at our little dining room table and worked the figures, what little there was of them, and then he closed his briefcase and headed for the door admitting to us that we clearly did not have the money now. I asked him how I could get in contact with him when I did have the money, and he turned about and looking over his glasses said, "We'll know. We'll know!"

It's a wonderful life! I would not know that a movie by that title was out there—let alone a classic—until years later when I would weep through my first viewing of it in Burgettstown.

Oh to be at Shell Beach!

I was also upset about the septic system. As I mentioned, the leach beds were filling with drain-off. Inquiring, I was told I had to dig around the tank and re-route the field tile, replacing the broken one in the process. That tank was buried six feet down and was three feet high in hard clay. The earth around it could not be shoveled, and I was told that if I didn't do it, I couldn't use my toilet, nor could I run water in the sinks or tub.

Me? I thought. Me?! No way! Get the backhoe in here to do it, since that was how they dug the hole in the first place. Besides, that clay is literally as hard as cement. It cannot be dug any other way.

The backhoe idea was a bad one, since there was no money, and they cost money. If I refused to dig around the septic tank, I would in a metaphorical sense be digging a grave for my career at the Bible school. So in any case, I would be digging something. I got a pick-ax from whom I don't remember, and I began to chop away at the clay. At the rate I was going, we would be looking at weeks of chipping away at this rock-like stuff, and with each passing day, I kept thinking how utterly impossible and how totally unfair this whole thing was.

No one came to help me. Do you ever have a problem that is all yours, and for whatever reason other people who know about it find it the better part of wisdom for them to keep their distance? "Clayitis" must have been highly contagious, or else the very idea of digging around a septic tank was repulsive, or maybe there was something about me and some lesson I needed to learn on my own.

I hadn't mentioned that on the other end of this septic tank fiasco was a well, which was dug into what was called red water. Red water is perfectly safe to drink, but it gives some people diarrhea. Mom did not get diarrhea. Timmy did not get diarrhea. Guess who got diarrhea but had no clue for days as to the why.

Clink, clink. My pickax hit something harder than the clay. A field-tile. I had arrived at the level where the tiles were. I had done it. I felt as if I had just won the Super Bowl, and I was the only player playing for my team against unspeakable odds. What an achievement! I came to believe that if I could fix this, I could probably do anything, if my resolve was there. It was that big of a deal for me.

And then, guess what. The diarrhea went away. I was getting used to the water.

And then, guess what. The Butler Area School District called with a job, part-time custodial work, but I took it! It eventually led to full-time and a regular pay check.

By now the weather was turning colder as autumn approached. I can remember making the trip to work... "To work"—Did you hear that? To work. I drove down 422 to my first custodial assignment, listening to the news on the radio, and things were looking up.

One early evening on my way to work going about 50 miles an hour, I noticed as I neared the exit I would take that my brakes weren't brak-ing. This problem was a light rain on an otherwise sunny afternoon. An-other time and another place, and I would be bemoaning my misfortune, but not that day. I was on my way to work! I used the emergency break to get the car to a local gas station, where the attendant found a stone that had lodged in the brake line, severing it and causing the break fluid to es-cape. He fixed it while I cleaned a school... and studied a little Hebrew.

This was a very good time as I viewed time of late.

The holidays were coming, and we were beginning to catch up with the bills.

It was October, 1972. What's so special about October, 1972? Do the math. October plus nine months equals July, 1973, my son Jim's birthday. I can remember Mom and I thinking a playmate for little Timmy would be a good idea. It was not as if we had a budget meeting over it or discussed it at length with secret ballot. We didn't need to. Our discussions were sometime so brief as to be almost incidental, so spontaneous as to betray a peaceful excitement about the possibility of another little one under foot.

I don't mean to make you cringe but all Mom and I had to do was toss the protection. What the heck? We want another kid.

I wasn't sure what I wanted, girl or boy. A girl might be nice since we had a boy, but a boy would make a more natural playmate, at least in my mind, for Timmy. Besides, having sons makes a man feel virile, or something. "My two sons." Sounds good. It has a certain ring to it.

Mom was carrying James, the bills were getting paid, I was working, and yes, we were going to move anyway, since the mortgage was still a little steep and the school would take the mobile home off our hands. We were moving to West Street. Things were not perfect by any means. West Street was for us half a house. The landlord's mother lived upstairs in what had been built as a single-family dwelling. The landlord built her a kitchenette and must have turned one of the bedrooms into a living room.

Meanwhile, downstairs, we turned the living room into our bedroom, the back foyer into Tim's bedroom, and the front foyer into a nursery for James, whom we nicknamed Jamie. By now a full-time custodial position had opened up, and I was gone all night from 11 PM to 7 AM I came home to sleep, while Timmy walked to and from kindergarten, and Mommy had little Jamie to care for.

Because the bills were being paid and my financial worries were disappearing, we even had medical insurance to pay for James's birth. I was feeling pretty great, but your Mom was not. One day, it seemed out of nowhere, she said, "I want to move." That's not a quote, because I can't remember her exact words and could not at the time appreciate her exact feelings. But she wanted to move. I didn't take it that she wanted to leave Butler, let alone Pennsylvania, but just West Street.

I won't analyze Mom except to say that the agony of the past year still lingered and yes, living in half a house has its drawbacks, to be sure. In effect, we had no bedrooms. That's how it felt, and that's how it looked. Whenever anyone visited, we had to invite them into a room with a bed, not a view. Guys might not mind this kind of thing, but women do mind it.

Our relationship was not perfect yet, either. I once brought a small battery-powered, AM radio to the bathtub with me to hear a complete Pirates baseball game. We had Roberto Clemente, you recall. That has to count for something. The truth is, an entire game. Things were not well between us.

Maybe somehow Mom sensed that a move into a real house, which was now affordable, with a backyard and cows for our two sons to look at, would be a healing balm on our relationship, or perhaps Mom just wanted to see cows. The cows grazed beyond the fence, behind our little house on McCandless Drive.

We moved to McCandless Drive, into a little farmhouse, in September, as I recall, 1975. We were only there three months before moving to Canonsburg, which is another chapter in my hunt for a career.

I do have memories of the place, the country road where the school bus stopped to pick up Tim for first grade and drop him off afterward; our first ringer-washer, which we had to use, because we were on a well and not city water; the cows; having a lawn to mow, even if I complained all the while I did it; and the night mom took an unannounced walk alone down that dark country road and disappeared into the night, while I had a diaper to change.

Doctor Garcia, my primary care physician, recommended part-time work when I became lightheaded one night and was unable to finish my shift. I loved my job. I had gone on a diet and was down to 165 pounds, but something wasn't right with my blood pressure, which was through the roof. I asked the Bible school one more time to hire me full-time so I would not have to do custodial work, but they could not, maybe because of what the board must have thought of me, maybe because of finances, maybe for another reason. I said that I would have to leave Butler.

"Do whatever you have to do," came the reply.

It was then that Pastor VanRiper, whom we affectionately called PVR, approached me with the offer of full-time ministry in Washington, PA, as his assistant pastor.

I accepted, of course. Later, I heard rumor that PVR stole me from the school. Go figure. We were nonetheless on our way to work in Washington—which was affectionately called "Little Washington"—and to live in the friendly town (and it was very friendly) of Canonsburg, where Perry Como was born. Canonsburg might have been the most polite and friendliest town on the planet, and we were going to call it home.

The Butler Eagle, on Wednesday November 19, 1975, related, "The part-time custodian has resigned to accept a full-time teaching position beginning Nov. 24 at Lighthouse Faith Bible School in Washington."

A Bathroom Without a View

Come aside by yourselves … and rest a while.
-- Jesus

I felt like I was on vacation. PVR seemed to sense that we needed a break, a rest, some kind of hiatus or sabbatical or call it what you will from the craziness that defined the past two years. He put us up in a cute townhouse apartment, very modern-looking with two bedrooms, if memory serves, and oh yes, a bathroom without a window.

Windows are drafty, but this bathroom hugged an inside wall and came with a built-in heating unit. A bath experience here was like being in a sauna, and the water never got cold. You can't imagine the hours I lay in that tub talking to the Lord and preparing for class as a teacher. It was a healing springs for me, not a physical thing, but an emotional and spiritual one, and I can only hope it had some positive value as well for Mom.

Pastor VanRiper's invitation to be part of the Lighthouse ministries was not out of the blue. We knew each other from my closing year in Butler. I had been one of a small group of faculty who made weekly trips to Little Washington to teach at the Bible school he had started there. Some denominational leaders had been put out with him for starting an independent ministry within five miles of an existing A of G church, which he had also started. But the Lighthouse ministries in Little Washington were not within five miles of the A of G church in Houston. (You can Google it.) He had broken no ethical rule, and I wasn't about to pretend that he had. So when his credentials as an Assembly of God minister were revoked, the other WPBI staffers decided to abandon him. I turned in my Assemblies of God credentials, chose to stay, and a relationship began.

I'm stupid, but maybe, just maybe, this time, the move was a smart one. Maybe, God was in that decision.

I don't know how I knew or sensed it, but I was thinking all along that our stay in Canonsburg would be brief. We were on a sabbatical of sorts. I think God must have known it and in His way said, "Come apart and rest a while." So we did, and so it was.

We arrived in Canonsburg just before the spring semester at the Lighthouse Faith Bible School, where I now was actually a teacher of some of the books of the Bible.

We set up house around Christmas, 1975, but my memories are of

33

warm spring air and pushing Jamie on the park swing while Timmy played in the sand. It is a memory of slow walks with Mom and lots of opportunity to talk and heal. It is a memory of sauna-type baths and deep prayer thought in preparation for the day's classes. It is a memory of eating out and trips to the store to buy what we now could afford. It is a memory of a small classroom of students that seemed to hang on my every word and of evening concerts, since PVR was a singer and he and Nadine maintained a dynamic music ministry, as they do to this day. We have a number of their albums.

It was during this time I had a chance to do something I wanted to do for some time. I wanted to write a thesis on the historical development of the perfect tense of the Koine Greek and its meaning in Scripture. I spent considerable time in the Washington and Jefferson College Library looking at books, primary source books in Greek and secondary source books which were translations of or commentaries on primary source books. I submitted the thesis for a Master of Bible Theology degree from International Bible Institute & Seminary, headquartered in Florida. Mom typed it up for me, as well as proof read it, for which I am grateful.

But all good things come to an end? The school closed its doors due to financial problems, after the close of the school year in 1976. And so I was once again out of a job. Pastor VanRiper chose to have the ministry continue paying for our rent in Canonsburg. This didn't last for long, since school ended late May or early June, and I stayed on temporarily as PVR's assistant, conducting the Wednesday evening Bible Study at the Lighthouse.

For a while—I don't remember for how long, but it wasn't for long—I took a job pumping gasoline at a local gas station in Little Washington to gather a little income. My only thought at the time was that pumping gas was not what I went to Bible school to do, nor did I travel hundreds of miles from home to tuck myself away in a Western PA town and disappear from sight behind a gas pump. One night when I counted down my cash, I discovered I was short by more than seventeen dollars, according to the pump meters. I had to pay this back to the station out of my own pocket. I don't recall how much money I was making, but seventeen dollars was a lot.

Then, one night while I was working at the pumps Mighty Joe Young, as I learned later they called him, came to visit me. He knew me from the Lighthouse, and he also knew that a small CCNA Church in Burgettstown was looking for a pastor.

Burgettstown, PA was about 20 miles north on route 18, not far away, and even though I had no idea what organization the CCNA was, aside from some remote, disconnected comment I may have heard over our years in Butler, I wanted to candidate that church.

Son, you may think your dear old dad a bit goofy but just before I met Joe Young, I started to have a recurring dream about a small white church. I think it was white, because the church I pastored in West Cape May was painted white. That was not mysterious. But what was of interest was with each recurrence of this dream, my interest in going back into pastoring intensified, until I was approaching desperation, and that was when Joe talked to me about Burgettstown.

We became a candidate for the church, I think, early in August 1976. And the vote—I cannot remember exactly what it was, and I heard that some voted who were not members, maybe mighty Joe Young. But the vote was favorable.

A win is a win.

Burgettstown would be a seven year stay. Basically, here is where two of you grew up.

We would stay there until Mother's day, May 9, 1983, when I would resign the church for our next move.

Of all Sundays to pick! But by now, however, you know how stupid I can be.

Under the Bubble

We judge of man's wisdom by his hope
–Ralph Waldo Emerson

It had to be one of the happiest days in recent years to be packing up our few belongings and heading into Burgettstown to pastor the Christian Assembly on Shady Avenue, just across the creek from the main road. I refer to Burgettstown as being under a bubble, because at the time —and this was before they built The Post Gazette Pavilion—the town seemed isolated from the world around it. The local folk in Burgettstown, in the old days, were miners primarily, and they were fiercely independent. The community was named for Fort Burgett, built here during the Revolutionary War by Sebastian Burgett. Each local community originally represented an entire ethnic group, such as on "Dago Hill." That name was spoken with affection, and not pejoratively. Slovan, just a few miles south, is where the Polish sector lived. When we arrived, the town boasted a population of just over 1,700 citizens, plus 11 saloons. This exceeded the legal limit by 10, since the rule was one bar per mile, and that was the length of route 18 as it wound its way through town.

That first Wednesday, as I walked down the short set of stairs into the basement off the sanctuary, I remember remarking to myself that I was home.

We all have many memories of Burgettstown since we were there for seven years which was the longest stay in any one ministry before or since. Here is where Timmy, age 7, and Jamie, age 3, were raised. Here is where I purchased a bag of lime and used it to paint white lines on a small patch of lawn next to the church's parking lot, turning this grassy area into a child-size football field. Here is where I was introduced to electronics and to the computer. I remember the Bell and Howell 11-book series on building a color TV set, which we borrowed from Rip, who lived up the hill behind us. We made it through two books and into the third before the interest in computers took center stage. I recall Tim's joy when his first computer, a Sinclair ZX81, finally arrived in the mail with just 1K of RAM. And Burgettstown is where we were gifted with our first color TV set which we later hooked up to the then popular VIC-20 computer and played for endless hours at games like Serpentine and Shamus.

I remember playing in the snow with James, and the walks with both boys to the ice-cream stand by the Presbyterian Church. My favorite memory is playing hide and seek with the boys in the state park. We would pick one of three separate paths that worked their way through the trees and among wild flowers and plants, some of them high enough to hide a small boy standing among them. The state park was a favorite retreat for me.

And do you remember Shorty's and Mary Ellen's swimming pool? Ralph "Shorty" Camp became one of my most trusted trustees, and Mary Ellen Camp was the church secretary. Both became life-long friends. We spent hours in their above-ground pool enjoying the summer air.

Like a newborn, there is a period of immunity. In ministry, it is the initial popularity you have that protects the new pastor from failing relationships, frustrated dreams, and yes, power struggles, where each leader seeks the vote for his or her vision for the church. Every ministry comes with a honeymoon period of about six months, when people are so glad you're there and so proud to call you pastor that you can do no wrong. I had one elder, who would later –I believe-- have at least some regret that we were still there. During that first month, however, he passed out copies of my Wednesday-evening Bible study notes to visitors as a way of inviting them back to hear me.

Yes, Burgettstown would provide its own brand of hurt, once the honeymoon ended. Some of the things that had happened so far seemed small change, compared to the price we would be asked to pay here, and neither Mom nor I could have ever expected it. I want to be careful not to go negative, because the cost of pastoring a church is in part the cost of all ministries.

One former pastor of the Burgettstown church told me that in another ministry—it was his experience—I would find circumstances more cooperative with what he believed God was calling me to do. With all deference, in looking back, I can politely disagree with him. Many of the people of this small town were the best thing that could have happened to us. It just took some time to see it, and of course, they had to get around to attending a service or two and meeting us. The Camps, for one, became life-long friends and were a support I genuinely missed in later ministries after we left. And who could possibly forget Butchie their son! Although Butchie was handicapped in what he could learn, he taught me that cheerfulness and a song can get us by.

There are seven years of memories, some of which are harder to put into words than others. My problem is twofold. One, I want to suggest that the job was what it was. Like any career, it comes with its challenges, its rewards, and its price. Pastoring should not be viewed as something exempt or separate and aloft from the normal flow of life. Pastoring means working with people. Some will come to love you, and some will come to disapprove of you, even hate you, though no one cares to admit that. Some will join and some will leave and the leaving is never pleasant.

Because pastoring involves people, it involves opinion and rumor. It involves defensive posturing, unfortunately, and detailed explanations of what you meant and what you did. It means exposing every action to public criticism. In Leadership magazine, written for Protestant clergy, there was a certain cartoon, with no caption necessary. The pastor and his family are seated at the dinner table in a house made completely of glass. The picture shows a couple probably from the church walking by and looking in while the pastor and his family eat.

Because pastoring involves people, it involves relationships, and therefore things like forgiveness and repentance and communication, things hard to do for some people for various reasons.

Some problems are unavoidable. The grass isn't greener elsewhere. They are also in the grass on the other side of the fence. They are part of life. They are part of growing up into the job. And where these experiences impacted Mom and our marriage, that too was not to be avoided.

I know, some might say, such and such would never have happened if I had chosen another career, and this almost seems plausible, since now I write computer programs for a living. The problem with this theory is that other things are not equal. For one, Mom and I, in particular, are a lot wiser, and some of the things that mattered intensely when we were younger are unimportant to us now. So let's be slower to judge and quicker to accept the experiences of life. Let's pick through them, in memories recalled to enjoy the good times and appreciate the lessons learned, and if possible, let's throw the rest away.

Two, some experiences were quite hurtful, and trying to relate them will not benefit anyone. Besides, since hurt means someone else is in the picture, and since I have absolutely no interest in showing anyone in a bad light, or even running the risk of doing that, I find it difficult to speak of these experiences.

I remember one man in the church which I came to hate briefly, before I came to appreciate him. I would not want to leave you with the hate and fail to lead you to the appreciation. And this was true in a sense over and over again. It is like some of the TV series that Mom and I watch. Enter a character whose initial impression is unfavorable. For the first season or so I detest him. I have told Mom that some of these parts in the series hang around too long, too much tension, too much negative vibration generated as a result of them. But as is the case again and again, something changes in the story to turn the Mr. Hyde into a Doctor Jekyll. And someone I hated becomes the most beloved character. Go figure.

If I were to begin to introduce someone in a poor light, and you were angered or hurt to hear about him, I would have to lead you through that and out into acceptance so that you could say goodbye to them in this narrative on an up note. I don't think I am that good a writer. I fear I would leave you with unresolved tension. Remember, the purpose behind this letter is to encourage you, not to leave you with unresolved anger, relived hurt, or painful regret.

Yes, in our ministry and marriage, Burgettstown made that big of a difference. Seven years in one place could not be overlooked in terms of our development and the aging process that makes one smarter and wiser, if it can.

My interest in being a pastor to a small group of people was guided by my then-notion of what true pastoring was about. My impression from reading Scripture, for right or wrong, was that pastoring meant caring about the spiritual well-being of people. This was not some vague abstract concept, but a concrete idea replete with Biblical examples: Paul weeping for the Ephesians, the prayer meeting for Peter at Mary's house while he was imprisoned, Jesus weary at the well. All spoke of personal involvement. There was here no administrative distance from the people. So I got involved. I attempted in a general sense to call each one friend, and when necessary would pray with them, counsel them, and teach them. I visited them by the hour, ate meals with them, held continued question and answer sessions after service.

I became close to the people not just of Christian Assembly but at times of Burgettstown and the surrounding communities. I think in wise reflection, I overdid it. I burned myself out by not recognizing a difference between my immediate family and my church family, by not recognizing that friendships are more unique and the honored role of a select few, by working until 2 AM, by praying all night or far into the night in preparing sermons and studies. My hospital calls were too frequent as well. Back then, someone would stay in the hospital for days, and I would try to see them at least every other day. The hospitals were, all but two of them, in Pittsburgh.

Memory begs, therefore, an audience for some topics and thoughts that I can relate: My hospital stay in the Washington General Hospital; the Charismatic Conference in 1979; legal matters and the church as a

501(c)(3) organization; teaching at Faith Community Seminary in Bethel Park, at The Washington Homes for Youth in 1982, and in other community based studies; preschool at CA; personal interests, from painting houses, to burning incense, to the birth of little Joshua.

It will not be possible for me to remember some things in sufficient chronological detail to justify telling them. I imagine I will shuttle back and forth across this seven year period weaving the threads of our family history that made up the tapestry of our stay in this pleasant and unforgettable town.

The Winter of My Discontent

*We are never more discontented with others than
when we are discontented with ourselves.
-- Henri Frederic Amiel*

The end of 1978 might have been one of the worst times for me. Before this, the summer of 1967 took first place. In 1967, I was working in the most undesirable job of my life, mowing lawns and emptying trash in a project for the City of Buffalo. The job was necessary if I was to return to Bible school. NBI required tuition and room and board up front, and I simply didn't have the money.

It was unbearable, and in a panic I ran away. I went by bus to Greenlane, to the NBI campus, for two days, seeking other employment, because any job was better than the one I had. Your Grandpa asked me to please get a round-trip ticket, but I told him that I would get a return ticket once there. He was visibly saddened by this decision.

When I reached campus, I found one of my favorite faculty members, Professor Grazier, painting a small utility shed, for extra income, I guess. I took the opportunity to interrupt him. I gave him a brief update that explained what I was doing there. Putting down his brush, he seemed to look at me with a stare that betrayed the wisdom of a man whose mistakes and regret seem to beg some chance at restitution, and said, "John, there are 49 things I would do differently if my dad were still alive."

I had to go home. Now! I returned home two days later, and the morning following my return, at 6 AM on June 27, your Grandpa King was found dead in his sleep.

Your Aunt Margaret, still a teenager at the time, was having her verbal wars with your Grandma King, and soon after Grandpa's death, she, your aunt, ran away. Uncle Bill, only 14 years old, was sent to Boston to live with family. The situation was that confused.

That was the year also that I asked Patty for her hand in marriage, and she wisely but sadly said, "No." Patricia was enjoyable to be with, but we were both too young for such a commitment. I couldn't see it. I have always been the practical type, and why date a girl if it isn't with a view to marriage?

It wasn't long before your Grandma King went into the hospital to have a major operation. When she did, I sat all alone at home. My only remaining companion was a huge gray rat that I spied one night rummaging about in the kitchen garbage. My mom instructed me to put out traps and kill it, but then I would be all alone without any visible companionship. I still had my faith in God, but that was now a distant theology, something I answered on a quiz once and got right. I suppose I was experiencing some form of social shock. I was emotionally numb. Worry assumes the possibility of crawling out of the ditch of an unresolved conflict. It figures the debt isn't so large that it cannot be repaid within a reasonable time frame. But when the ditch is deep and your income cannot begin to address your need, worry serves no purpose any longer. You simply sit and stare. For now, I couldn't see how any bills were going to be paid, or how my mom would adjust on her return home.

Oh, I let my wild pet live.

We found Aunt Margaret, who under the circumstances had no problem coming back, but the refrigerator was empty. I had been living on cans of pork and beans, seasoned with ketchup, a favorite when you haven't a clue how to cook. I did return to mowing lawns but at this point nothing mattered accept trying to collect a few bucks for food and utilities.

Your Grandpa King had had a very weak heart. No one had doubted it when the doctor diagnosed it and called him a walking dead man. But that could not assuage my guilt. I still wondered if he would have lived longer, had I not taken the trip to Eastern PA. For years I believed I played a major role in my father's death, and I am not sure yet of my innocence.

The year 1978 ended worse than this. It was then that for the second time in my life I planned to run. Upon reflection it wasn't my proudest moment but it had become the true psychological indicator that I had reached the end of my tether.

Unlike the summer of '67, I cannot point to specific events that burdened me with increased responsibilities. The hole in which I had found myself in 1967 that I couldn't seem to crawl out of was dug by a backhoe of unfortunate circumstances that took large scoops of my security away. But by the winter of 1978, we had been in Burgettstown two years, the honeymoon having ended after the first few months, and the situation that made me so uncomfortable was like a hole dug with a spoon slowly and gradually over that year and a half. I only can guess that since I didn't sense the ground beneath me caving in, I was slowly sinking emotionally, and at no time was I overwhelmed with any new event. Each challenge had a possible solution, though I awoke that year's end to find that none had been solved, and now I had to look skyward to see the ground level.

I remember mulling over the analogy of a boat with three holes in it. One hole represented a bad relationship with the church board, another represented a bad relationship with the Mrs.. and a third represented a poor relationship with God. The first could come about by a power struggle, everyone wants their own way; the second one, through circumstances that cause two people to drift apart, which I will relate shortly; and the third, through any kind of sin. All three reveal a lack of communication so essential to one's mental and emotional health. I think these three holes were in the bottom of my boat and at first I thought I could stay afloat by staying focused on my ministry. I thought I would just keep bailing water. I have since learned the obvious, that it doesn't work that way.

Much later, on an application for ministerial credentials, I was asked to give my response when the minister encounters "resistance from: a church board, individuals, etc." Oh that I had had the answer to this question then! What worsened my relationship with the church board was an unresolved legal matter that surfaced when I took leadership to get the church on track with the IRS. It turned out that the building was privately owned, through the fault of no individual. The church had been purchased through private capital, which was paid back, but the name on the deed was never corrected to reflect congregational ownership. It was still the personal property of a few individuals, one of whom had died and whose interest had been passed on to his children. Some other "owners" no longer lived locally.

"The law is a horrible business," said Clarence Darrow. One signer of the original deed was living locally but seemed to be avoiding me. It was—I can only guess—as if I were the thief in the night come to rob him of something. It is true that church property, regardless of legal matters or signatures on deeds, is cherished by some folk as much as they cherish their own homes. It must have been obvious to some that I didn't share the feeling. All I wanted to do is let the people in and let them all feel at home while there. This attitude typically gets a preacher in trouble, I found out. So board meetings tensed up.   On reflection, I should have befriended those guys more, spent time with them, planning things together while, for the sake of the minister who would follow me, not giving up the pastorate or its importance in the government of God. I couldn't find the way.

The Sunday School leadership was also put out with me, but with the lack of communication it was never clear what happened to upset them. I gathered only that Mom and I were different than the previous pastor and his wife. A few teachers were only struggling with adjustment. There must have been things done before that some now missed, and some new things that some now didn't appreciate. Personality clashes, not doctrinal differences, seem to rock a boat already taking on water.

I missed Shell Beach. I missed the seagulls, too. They were part of that peaceful retreat that now was years and miles away.

My first mistake with Mom—and I use the word first only as a jumping off point—was that I failed to successfully defend her from what one might call the unexpected assault on her own ministry or role as a pastor's wife. Church people have an opinion on this topic, which is generally based on previous ministries, not on Bible verses. While I thought over my response, which lacked a certain spontaneity, Mom retreated, I believe, into the quiet security of a mother's world with her children.

I am sorry, sons. Your Mom seemed to be emotionally leaving me, and I take responsibility for that now. But at the time, I felt neglected. Here I am with all my woes and problems, and now this.

I tried one night to break the silence. It was not as if we didn't talk; we did. Our chief subject of common interest was you, because nothing ever lessened our love for you or the initial thrill of having you with us. That goes for both of you, Tim, Jim. Josh, you were not in the picture yet. But this particular night the subject was romance, and I was having an impossible time understanding the definition of it. I recall Mom in frustration say something like, "It's a warm fire in the fireplace!"

We did have a fireplace, but there was a galvanized pipe protruding through the floor where a grate should be. So I removed the pipe and revitalized the fireplace. There. Now she has a fire in a fireplace. But it somehow wasn't romantic. I missed some detail. Maybe it was like Marie on Everyone Loves Raymond would say about cooking, that you have to add the love. That was getting a bit difficult, because the spontaneity was being replaced with the mechanics. Perhaps the last ten years of one difficulty after another was catching up to us, because we didn't face them at the time as much as move away when things got too hard for us to deal with them. Does this sound vaguely psychological familiar? You read my profile. But moving seemed a solution, and no doubt it was, on occasion. Now, however, no one was moving. I had a church to pastor! We were where we should be. And where was that?

Herman Melville once said, "It is not down in any map; true places never are."

Mom use to say, "You are working for God, not the church!"
Maybe so...

And then there was need for burning incense.

Mark Twain once said, "I have been through some terrible things in my life, some of which actually happened." The need to mask some foul order lofting up from the basement was real for all of us. We lived on the side of a hill and above us they were strip mining. Strip mining takes off the top 80 feet or so of soil and moves it aside to get at the coal that is underneath, rather than actually digging a mine. This usually means underground water wells are found and need to be routed or dealt with in some way. One of these underground streams went down the side of our house, to empty into another stream flowing along Shady Avenue into the creek. A former owner had blocked this flow, so now the water found another route, through our basement. And this water was sulfurous, so it stunk like rotten eggs. The town authorities were glad to have the sulfur there since it was a natural sanitizer. We heard a rumor that one family up the hill above us made life easier for themselves by running their sewage directly into this stream. Who knows if this was true or if some waste might have found its way into our basement. Disgusting!

The flow through our basement at times was real enough for me to build a small bridge out of wood planks and bricks so mom could reach the washing machine without going wading. Our washing machine did rust through at the bottom. Remember the ringer-washer on McCandless Drive? We gifted that to a widow and bought an electric washer, which now sat on the opposite bank of our rivulet. It wasn't until Shorty became a trustee that this problem was resolved. Until then, Mom burned incense just to hide the smell.

While I am pointing out problems I might mention my workload. In order to make ends meet, I took odd paint jobs and some teaching opportunities to earn extra money. One trustee told me, perhaps jokingly, that it was their job to take care of us, so they kept us needy. We needed to supplement our $250 a week check.

During the course of our stay in Canonsburg and Burgettstown, we had replaced the '72 Maverick with a Chevy Nova, and that was replaced by a Chevy Malibu Wagon, and that by a Toyota Tercel. There were two reasons for all the new cars. One, I didn't like driving an old car, since I did a lot of traveling in the tri-state area between South Pittsburgh and Steubenville, Ohio. So I got a new car every 60 or 70 thousand miles, and that meant an ongoing car payment that kept going up and up, because I had to roll the balance for the last car into the loan for the next. That meant I was always paying on at least two cars at any given time. Two, I learned to hate driving on ice, so I needed front wheel drive.

I would be gone for hours. I would be teaching in a Christian Book Store, where they had set up class for me in a back room. Students paid 5 dollars a piece for the privilege of hearing me talk. Or I would be teaching at Faith Seminary in Bethel Park, PA, south of Pittsburgh, on a weekly basis during the school year. Or I would be making hospital calls at Pittsburgh's Mercy Hospital, Presbyterian Hospital, or Children's Hospital.

I actually developed a sort-of reputation as a Bible teacher who knew some Greek! This later would open the way for me to teach at the 1979 Charismatic Conference at Duquesne University in June. But for now it simply meant being away hoping to collect a few bucks to help with the bills.

I was also asked to serve on the board of Trustees for the Lighthouse Ministries, since I had served them back in '75. They had a debt to that ministry which exceeded all sources of income, and people were leaving. Looking back, the reasons are now clear. But at the time the board needed to dissolve legally and pay off all church debts. Mom and I had a credit-card debt of over $1,700 that seemed overwhelming, until the board elected to award us back pay for the year we served on staff. Mom and I used the money to wipe the credit card clean, making a vow never to use it again. What a laugh!

This provides only a glimpse into the past, a glimpse that still leaves a lot of questions unanswered about my relationships and how they were drifting apart. In addition, I felt estranged from God. I missed your mother's affection, and each time we talked over any issue in which either one of us took a personal interest, it seemed to end in hurtful argument followed by painful silence. I wasn't praying like I should have been, I guess. I was even phobic about the possibility of losing my family. Unreasonable? Yes, but real to me,nonetheless.

It all came to a head after Christmas, 1978. Sometime around the new year, I was in the basement working with paint remover. We had an old piano I was refinishing. I had been a house painter, but I did not refinish furniture. I also knew that paint remover fumes were not good to inhale. I remember looking up and seeing you boys at the head of the stairs showing an interest in what Daddy was doing. I shooed you off telling you to close the door behind you and you obeyed. Looking back, I am thankful to God and family that that was not the last time I would have to see your inquisitive faces. The sight of you standing there at the top of the basement stairs will be with me forever. Those could have been my last words to you if I had succumbed to the vapors that were all around me. There may have been no tomorrow if the fine particles of old paint and remover, which I was sanding off that piano, with an electric sander, and which I was breathing in, had filled my lungs with its poison.

I was a bit disoriented not because of paint remover but because of everything else going on around me. The piano refinishing was just an example of how disconnected I had become from my real responsibilities. All the while, I was thinking of making a solo visit to New Jersey. I was not planning a trip to Shell Beach, which might have been a blessing, that blessing contingent on also bringing the family with me. But I was planning to go alone. I was leaving in the morning, and no one even knew it.

I had never before made such a decision without conversing with someone over it. This was a first in that regard. Not even Mom knew. No one knew except God. I reasoned that I would talk to our former pastor, who married us, and he would help me get refocused. I reasoned that I would inform Mom once there. I assumed I was going by car, since I had no bus fare. I wouldn't have gone by train or plane. I needed to get out first and think through some details, so I got in the car and drove to Pittsburgh. I really wanted to get away, and the thought of leaving my sons didn't cross my mind.

When someone is depressed, they likely will not think through the implications of their actions. People in that frame of mind are filled with contradictions, exaggerations, and rationalizations. The Charismatic Conference I had been invited to for the coming year was also not in my thoughts. I also had an evening Bible study to prepare for, because it was a Wednesday. That, I thought, I would forgo studying for.

This was totally unlike me. Was it the paint remover? I don't know. I only know that while driving around the city, I began to sense what I would call an ice cream headache. I didn't think anything about it, although it grew worse by the minute. I decided to return home since it was approaching 7 PM, and I had a Bible study to conduct. It almost seemed like I was drifting in and out of lucidity.

I drove to the church and collected my notes for that evening's study, even feeling as bad as I did, and I went to the podium to arrange them. One sheet left my hand and floated to the floor. I reached down to pick it up, and I couldn't! Grandma King always said that if you were having a heart attack, you would not be able to raise your hands above your head. That was my first thought, so, I lifted both arms above my head. No heart attack, I felt relieved.

One moment I don't care if I live, and the next I don't want to die. This is the ambivalence of a man sick with whatever I had. I reached down again to pick up the sheet of notes, and once again failed at it. I went home to talk with Mom.

That must have been the first sensible thought I had had in days.

Mom drove me straight to the emergency room at the Washington General Hospital, where I sat in the waiting area until one of the trustees, Fred, arrived. Before we left, Mom sent out notice that Wednesday Evening study had been canceled. When Fred got the message, he came to the hospital to find me still waiting, and he moved into action on my behalf. The medical team didn't get the message, but now finally did, that I was having a heart attack. At least that is how Fred diagnosed it.

They brought me to a table in the ER and hooked me up to an IV drip. I understood, one of the nursing staff was having difficulty finding a pulse. Upon reading a very low pulse, they decided to keep me overnight in Cardiac ICU.

One family in the church later informed me that had I faith in God for healing, I would not have been there. I disagreed, and still disagree. I spent four glorious days in intensive care, and two in post-coronary, studying for the conference, and what was more, reuniting with Mom.

I fell in love with her all over again.

Hospital stays must do that for me. The heart monitor would register a sudden leap in my pulse when Mom showed up in the doorway of the room. One day, I thought she wouldn't be coming, since a snow storm was threatening to keep her away, but she showed up, to my joy.

That Sunday, my last day in the hospital, was January 7, the day the Pittsburgh Steelers beat the Houston Oilers for the right to attend Super Bowl XIII, which they won. This playoff game only helps me fix the date. The real Super Bowl win was the complete turnaround within me, during one short week in the hospital. I came away with renewed interest in ministry, a little more wisdom in knowing what was important, a brand new excitement for my two little boys. It was a sort of honeymoon, since I had not spent as much time with Mom as I did that week, while lying in a hospital bed, preparing a study for the conference on the dynamic of true Christian love.

The conference wouldn't occur until June but I was ready for it on the second week of January. I came home to incense and perhaps a disappointed board member or two—I can't really know—and all the problems that were there before. But, maybe for the first time in years, I came

50

home to my family.

Vegetable Soup

If my grandmother were a food,
she would probably be vegetable soup.
She is made up of a lot of different ingredients,
and when you put them all together,
it creates something warm and wonderful.
--Joanne Thompson

The next four years would be productive in terms of my career as a pastor. The church was growing in numbers; my teaching ministry was fulfilling to me, whether in a book store or at the seminary in south Pittsburgh. It was my connection in 1979 with Doctor Jim Laine, President of Faith Seminary in Bethel Park PA, that opened the opportunity for my teaching at the Conference at Duquesne University in June.

Enter WHY, the Washington Home for Youth, an organization that provided a young social worker and his wife to take in a half dozen dependent and neglected teen boys—There were similar homes for girls—and provide them a home life. It was a kind of foster home for teen boys. I had the privilege of bringing a weekly Bible study to the boys who expressed an interest in it. Yes, we encouraged such an interest by placing the study in the middle of general study time. So a boy could avoid that hour and a half of study time by joining us. The study we agreed upon was the life of Jesus, a simple chronological look at where Jesus went during His adult life. We would interject a few thoughts as to the why of His decisions as He journeyed from one end of Palestine to the other. I was excited to see the boys' interest pique, as if we were watching a mystery movie or a drama, as it unfolded and the pieces to the historical puzzle of Christ's life were brought into place. Later I would write a hundred-page narrative based on this study.

These years were filled with word studies, which became the content of many Wednesday-evening Bible Studies. I would spend hours studying one Biblical term, researching it in a number of resource books. In an effort to know what actually was written, to get as close as I could to the thought behind the word, as a Bible writer might have understood it, to capture some emphasis, to confirm an existing view, or to learn a new one, I researched verse after verse late into the night, night after night.

Teaching was and is me, and I am good at it. It also explains a lot about my personality that might level the balance bar, after all the nega-

53

tive reports I have been piling on one side. I know I should never consider running for political office, but there is much about me that lends itself admirably to teaching, regardless of the subject. One problem for me results from that subject, the Bible. I don't go into prophecy or trying to predict the immediate future, nor do I spend my time theologizing or trying to figure God out. I tend to talk life and have even been accused of being more psychological than Biblical. People in the know can agree that the Bible is psychological, both in tone and content, and the Bible is good at it, too. In fact, the Baptists refer to its teachings as important "for life and conduct."

As a teacher, one of my greatest assets is that I am human and imperfect, and my experiences have been my teacher. Openness and honesty become my greatest characteristics. Put another way, I am not the fisherman but one of the fish, and I didn't know what a hook was until I got caught on one. Now, I can explain hooks to other fish.

Sunday Services were not my favorite, however, because they included elements of ceremony that were culturally interpreted. Every church has ritualized some approach to a Sunday service that dictates how things are done and when. This tends to diminish the emphasis that should be placed on teaching the Bible. Changing this approach is dangerous for a pastor especially if he is new to the church. First of all, he would anger people to the point that Sunday morning couldn't exemplify worship anymore. There would be too much hurt and anger to allow it.

The major problem he faces is that the ritual is required to define the service; things are never done on a hit-or-miss-or-anything-goes basis. Disorganization sounds spiritual to some, but it does not achieve that result. Services are seldom led by God even if some Pentecostals claim as much when they allege that God, not man, is somehow in control of things. Even if God were in charge, the theology knows Him to be a God of order.

But God isn't in control of everything that happens in all churches. That should be obvious. If He were, the church wouldn't be so divided. God has a voice in all Christian churches when His word is read or sung, when something is said by a pastor that edifies a congregant, when two believers support each other's decision to live right. God does not, however, make all the decisions, as if church leadership was without the ability either to plan something on a Sunday morning or to carry out that plan. Church leadership has traditionally vied for the right to lead.

Sunday service was to me a planned service which culturally did not treat the study of the Bible with enough emphasis. There were announcements and testimonies and offerings and special recognitions, all of which take time from an hour-long service. I considered singing very important, but too often songs were planned out of necessity, more than prepared with inspiration.

Sunday morning church service to me was like a bowl of vegetable soup consisting mostly of hot water. There is some nourishment there, but it isn't "soup," as advertised. Sunday evening for me was even more watered down, because of the short time I had to prepare for it. I seldom prepared two services ahead, so Sunday evening service was not in my thoughts until after lunch Sunday afternoon. So I maintained these bits of Christian culture as part of my job while slipping the word studies in as chunks of vegetables in an otherwise weak soup.

The nice thing about Christian Assembly in Burgettstown was that it allowed me to be me. I held Bible studies in private homes as well as the Wednesday-evening one at the church. I had small groups going in a number of locations. I held studies and prayer meetings in Langeloth, Racoon, Florence, and Cross Creek among other places, and there was no resistance from church members, with the possible exception of one elder who felt the church building should be utilized more. His criticism could be viewed as honest and constructive.

I didn't realize at the time that the Burgettstown church group was as a culture—or as a congregation—relatively cooperative. People in Washington County would years afterward stand out in my memory as some of the most friendly and supportive of all church members I had worked with over the years.

They sometimes got hurt, but not vengeful. If something didn't set well with one of them, he or she might disappear for a while, attend another church, or just stay home, and yes, it might gain public sympathy, but there was no attempt at organizing the pastor's removal. It might have been a subcultural quirk of an economically depressed area. It might have been because we were among folk of humble origins. Perhaps, we benefited there because the church was not primarily hi-tech administrative types who naturally interpreted discontent as a need to fire someone. Or maybe the community idea was already a part of them. People from the Presbyterian church were very close friends with individuals in Christian Assembly.

Whatever the reason, no one seemed to think it unnatural for me to visit someone from another congregation that was without a pastor, or to hold a study in a Presbyterian church in a nearby town. And I enjoyed every moment of it.

I visited people. I guess I did this because pastors which I looked up to did that, or maybe I just missed the good old days when pastors like doctors made house calls. I also interpreted Scripture to be saying that I should. It seemed to me that some verses of Scripture were beyond mis-interpretation when they more than suggested or implied that I should care about people and get involved on a deeper level than just a Sunday Morning handshake. Their meaning to me could not be clearer or sim-pler. It said what it said.

So when I read, "Pure religion and undefiled before God and the Fa-ther is this, To visit the fatherless and widows in their affliction," (em-phasis added), I did just that. Throughout the course of our stay in Bur-gettstown I visited the widows, which included elderly women who nev-er married. It might seem strange for someone like myself who almost prides himself on being a slave to exact meanings of Bible verses to inter-pret some Scriptures so loosely when it comes to caring. A woman over 59 and without a husband was in the category of widow. I cannot believe God made a distinction there. They were like mothers to me.

On one such visit, I discovered that Anne lived in a small home that was well aerated. There were eighth- to quarter-inch cracks around some of the windows, letting in the cold air. Since winter was coming, I made a trip to the local hardware store and bought the necessary equipment to storm-proof all the windows of her little bungalow, at church expense. I considered that appropriate. This was the also church member to whom we gave the ringer-washer. As a footnote I might mention the bee hive we removed when the little creatures decided to live in with her.

This is not intended as a boast, but an explanation of what was and is important to me in ministry, and I think this is also one reason I gener-ally do not qualify as a modern-day pastor. The modern approach seems to be more to administer and to delegate away such responsibilities as caring. This can be a very good reason for the change which I found diffi-cult to adjust to. Modern churches, because of their size and the complex-ity of need in a modern world, would overburden today's pastor and burn him out. Bible seminaries do not train counselors, but administra-tors and theologians, while the task of counseling is a specialty, like ev-erything else these days, given to trained counselors.

In a Biblical form of church governing, deacons did the visiting, and one might argue that such was not the pastor's work. I could not be sure, so I got involved with people in an effort to care enough to make a posi-tive difference. In any event, that was how I viewed the pastorate, not re-alizing the affect it would ultimately have on me. Years later, I would seek a happy medium between the two extremes, but while in Burgettstown, I continued to befriend an entire congregation, even if they didn't see it that way. It was my desire and my attempt. I have since learned that the word pastor is difficult to define in the Bible.

One day I visited an elderly man, Charlie, who was digging a trench to bring town water up to his home. He lived in what we might consider poverty, with his wife and their pet dogs. They shared a two-room home that until recent times had had a path to an outhouse. Bringing running water into the house was a huge deal for both of them. I showed up in a business suit, because that is what pastors generally wore back then. When I saw him laboring away with pick-ax and shovel, I simply jumped into the trench and began to help, suit and all. Mom wasn't happy about the suit. It needed dry cleaning, and fast. But I did what I do and enjoyed it.

I had one of my biggest regrets that involved Charlie, and I would do things differently if I could. Charlie requested a visit when he was dying of cancer. We had left Burgettstown by then and were living in Sharon, PA, about 70 miles north. I was painfully reluctant at the time to return, and I thought that I had a legitimate excuse. I was busy with my new duties. That excuse wouldn't work for me now, if I had the chance to relive the moment.

Pastoring meant people to me, and when I ignored that connection and tried to make it more administrative or more clerical, I couldn't get into it. Pastoring for me meant caring about people, whether it meant digging a trench or staying up half the night in prayer for someone in the hospital. It meant one, two, three hour visits. Three hours was a little over the top unless the visit included a swimming pool and a meal. Pastoring meant being available when I was needed.

I actually installed two phone lines in the house, and at times I was talking on both lines at the same time to two different people. That is over the top!

But pastoring also meant knowing when to hang up and that was not always easy for me.

Friendships

A friend is someone who knows the song in your heart
and can sing it back to you when you have forgotten the words.
--Bernard Meltzer

We did have our friendships over the years, and these were very special. What needs to be said is that on my part, they were not always just naturally developing relationships. At times, I needed a friend, so I went out and found one.

These relationships were the flip side of my ministerial coin. I needed someone to care about me, or to provide needed emotional support to me. Few people could qualify for this, because few people had the emotional resources sufficient to share a little caring with me without becoming very needy themselves. Also since potential friends are not professional counselors, they know nothing about transference of affection and intimacy issues, which destroy friendships. I needed people who could get close always and only as friends. I needed people who were wise enough and healthy enough to allow openness and honesty, to encourage such closeness without redefining the relationship as something ethically or morally questionable. I needed persons with whom I could be totally comfortable, say what I wanted to say, and be what I wanted to be, without their being anxious for my stability. I needed persons who could offer me the same definition of friendship I offered them, and somehow we both knew that, and that the friendship was a true one. I needed a hug without words when tearful, a listener when I really needed to hear myself.

I didn't quiz or analyze potential friends. They just happened after I stole the first Christian handshake. Probably the only observable requirement was that possible friends needed to be married, so that the friendship could be a couple's thing.

Generally, I didn't use friends as counselors, as much as I used their pools and barbecue pits as tools for relaxation and time off, or their game boards as a focal point for socializing or just plain laughing together. But on occasion I needed advice and they were there for me.

One such occasion was over the legal matter of moving the ownership of the church property from private hands to those of the congregation, and here is where I can get friendship-specific and name names. I went to Shorty and Mary Ellen Camp for help, support, anything and everything they could do as friends to keep me focused and at peace with my decisions. I had to research the matter in the County Bureau of Records. I had to visit persons whose names appeared on the deed and argue for signing the property over to the church proper. I met with other pastors, corresponded with the IRS, and worked with lawyers, all of which required a second pair of eyes for reviewing or correcting things. If Shorty and Mary Ellen had not been friends already—but they were—they certainly would have become friends for life after this. They had no choice. Getting rid of me was now impossible, short of a restraining order.

We developed in earlier ministries other friendships worth mentioning: Denny and Amy Thompson, and Gary and Jan Davis, both while in Butler; Pastor George and Nadine VanRiper, in Little Washington; and there were to be others later. Each friendship was unique and special. Each friendship had its own dynamic. Each one had its own value to me, and each one would last well into the years and beyond the locale where we met.

I think the Thompsons' and Davises' helped us keep equilibrium during our Butler years, because they provided a friendship that helped us to laugh through troubles. They gave us evenings of pure relaxation and a time away from worries, and they knew (from what they had to deal with in those days) what Mom and I were actually living through. You kids would fall asleep on the living room carpet or some piece of furniture in one of their homes, young, small bodies draped over anything soft, while we grownups played board games late into the night and on into the early morning. We sometimes went from having fun to wanting to pray and that was fun, too.

Because of friends, Mom and I found the encouragement to face the next day. That may sound overstated, but like taking three deep breaths before diving under water, being with friends, in its own unnoticed and magical way, did in fact keep us from drowning in our problems. We didn't need to know the psychology behind having close friends during the hard times. We didn't need to get counseling to tell us, or read books on the importance of hanging around people who can laugh with us or, better yet, make us laugh or, even better yet, deny us the right to forget how to laugh. Friends are simply friends. Like a good meal they come with all the vitamins and minerals you need even if you don't realize it.

I was emotionally close to an entire congregation. I already said that. There were many like Daisy or Charlie or Vera or Sister Sarracino or Gazella or Anne or John—and there were others—who will forever have a special place in my heart. No doubt about it. What made these individuals special was their consistency through the years. While others moved up and down in how they felt about Mom and me, these few did not. They hung in there with their prayers and encouragements.

Daisy was a bonus. She alone could have summed up the total reason for our being in town, keeping a small otherwise unimportant church open. One afternoon, Daisy walked in and sat down. I was there preparing for Sunday, probably. I don't remember other than to know that this was my custom. When I saw her, I approached her, wondering if I could be any help. She began by telling me that she didn't know why she had come in. It was so unlike her, she had no explanation. She thought maybe I did.

I did. People do things and later cannot explain adequately why, and the younger they are, the more likely this will happen. But walking into a church when it was not their intent or custom or forethought sounds positively mysterious. I maintain without hesitance that this is just like the providence of God, to direct a person in such a way, to move them beyond their own plans.

Daisy never stopped coming and she has become a dear friend and support for Mom and me.

I apologize here and now for not remembering all the names and listing them in this honor roll from Burgettstown, but these friends didn't do what they did for us for the recognition. They were not there week after week because I promised to mention their names anywhere. They were who they were, and lived out their kindness, as spontaneously as breathing. I just had the good fortune—the providence—of getting to know them.

I mention all of this to give you necessary insight into what made me what I was at the time, how I related to people and why there existed at times a conflict between family time and so-called church work. Right or wrong, it was what it was.

Am I different today? Decidedly. Now my entire focus is immediate family. But back then, I hadn't learned yet where along that continuum to conduct my calling. I hadn't figured out a lot of things. I did lack some wisdom. Perhaps the Camps had us over for pool parties to pull me away from my work and into some family time, because one of my fondest memories is splashing in their pool with you, my two sons.

The Bad Guys

People who set up repressive machinery always think it's going to be directed against the Bad Guys (whoever they think the Bad Guys are) and never against themselves.
--Tom Parsons

Who were the bad guys? After all, not all of our woes could have been because of finances, could they? Is it possible that all would have been right with our world had we inherited a million bucks?

No.

Aside from the possibility of doing tons of work gratis, we still dealt with people and challenges that money could not have solved. You knew that without my saying it.

People did hurt us but I cannot start naming names here for many reasons. First, my memory is gone when it comes to the particulars of broken relationships. Maybe it is true that we choose to forget. Maybe forgiveness really works.

Secondly, I would have to analyze people from our past as to what they might have or might not have meant by what they said or did, people that we think hurt us. Analysis is not my forte, and even of it were, I would need to analyze my role in all of it, and self-analysis is a risky business. (But I don't mind the risk when I am talking only about me.)

Thirdly, I am not exactly sure who the bad guys were. Mom and I have had apologies offered us by individuals wanting our forgiveness, people that we never knew had anything to do with the terrible things that happened.

A fourth idea is Biblical. Whoever is without sin can cast the first stone. Sorry, I cannot cast the first stone.

My biggest reason—and the only one I need for not naming names— is that I don't want to shoot myself in the foot with that loaded gun, and that is what would happen if I cocked the trigger. One seldom hurts the hurter as much as he hurts himself and his family by becoming vindictive.

If I could use a way-out-there illustration, it is as if a church board were to draw up a constitutional change to make it easier to remove undesirables from office only to have the amendment come back to bite them when someone else uses it to remove them from office. I have seen it. Whenever I held an office that gave me the right to advise, I always recommended simple documents. Don't try to legislate the act of Christian love, which should be spontaneous, not rigid or programmed through law. Try to use reasonableness and some sensitivity, with wisdom, when dealing with one another. I still think it is a good idea in all our relationships.

So, there are no bad guys?

I guess not.

From time to time we all play the part of a bad guy. We all do bad things to people. Sometimes unknowingly. Sometimes, sad to say, with planned precision we hurt others. Sometimes we get away with it, because our plan was foiled before it could succeed, and we look back thankfully at failure. Sometimes our tracks are erased and people go on thinking how nice we always were.

And sometimes very good people, who otherwise are candidates for sainthood, do something totally out of character. It is the one flaw in an otherwise perfect life. When they have opportunity to relive their decision, they do so with such regret they beg forgiveness from God and man. These people have the right to continue living without the grief of unresolved wrong.

What is craziest of all is that sometimes the person who hurt me yesterday is a good friend today. That makes psychological sense. If two people who are fighting start communicating their hurt and their anger to one another, the hurt and anger tends to die. They plant a seed, so to speak, and the fragrant flower of understanding grows where weeds of rationalized conceptions once flourished. That is not the best way to put it, but sometimes we get so put out with someone that we feel we have to speak up and say something. Our initial idea is self-justification. We want to tell them off, but sometimes we make the mistake of real communication. Someone stops yelling and starts listening, even though they didn't learn that art. The atmosphere changes. Storm clouds start to move away and the bright sun of forgiveness and "I'm sorry" comes out.

Put away your umbrella. You don't need protection or a defense anymore from nastiness or verbal assault. Embrace the sunlight of a new beginning with someone you thought would hate you forever.

Mom and I have seen this happen with person after person. The friendships I mention above were named because this never happened between them and us. They were close from day one and never moved away. But other individuals—and there are a few who could be placed in this chapter—drove over some rough spot on the road to a fond and memorable relationship with us.

64

I have since reconciled with a number of the players in this mini-drama known as my life as a minister. Today, I can call some of them friends. Others who have preceded me to whatever awaits all of us after this life I can look back with memory's eye and actually say, "I was glad to have met you."

Thomas Jefferson, when an old, private letter of John Adam's, attacking Jefferson in print, showed up sometime after they had retired from public life, remarked, "It would be strange indeed, if, at our years, we were to go an age back to hunt up imaginary, or forgotten facts, to disturb the repose of affections so sweetening to the evening of our lives." My sentiments exactly.

Yes, I suppose there are one or two people that would avoid us even in heaven, if they could. That's if I don't see them first and have a chance to run up and surprise them with a hug.

Fondest Memories

Every man's memory is his private literature.
--Aldous Huxley

The tapestry of our life was interwoven with good times as well. These are fond memories: walking the tracks hand in hand with Mom talking over our next move; playing ball with you in the lot across the road, son against son and Dad on both sides; playing the new video games with you on our first colored TV set, sometimes by the hour; splashing in the Camp's pool, which temporarily removed my pot belly; playing hide and seek in the State park along a mile trail which included three-foot-high wild plants and other natural hiding places for young boys.

The railroad tracks ran behind the church and could easily be reached from the far end of the church property in the back. The friendly thing about these tracks was their unevenness. The rails often were not parallel along a stretch of track that ran between Burgettstown and Slovan. The cross ties were in places, as if someone had spread out giant pick-up sticks so they wouldn't be piled on top of one another and then pressed them in place. Some seemed placed deeper in the track bed than others.

One could walk those tracks without fear of being struck by a train, because no train could chug along them at more than 5 miles an hour. We would know it was coming and step aside, waving hello to an engineer or two. Besides, seldom did we ever see a train. So Mom and I could walk to Slovan and back along the tracks, talking strategy, if we had a problem to solve or a matter that bothered one or both of us. Or we could just enjoy planning your future, whether it meant affording a toy or a picnic.

The tracks in some odd or unusual way replaced Shell Beach for me, since I couldn't get to the Jersey shore. Probably by now they had finished the clean up of that beach, which we found on a later return. But we had tracks at least in Burgettstown, and we walked them often, a few times a week, I think. When you follow an old rail line off-road and into the woods, you leave people. When you leave people, for the time being, you leave the problems they present.

The tracks for me were romantic, a word on which it seems I couldn't get a handle. When I would go on a business trip, usually a District-wide meeting for the churches in our organization, I got to eat well. They expensed a fancy restaurant meal, and I knew Mom and you were home with hot dogs. So I said, "I love you" to Mom with a take-home dinner of whatever I had ordered. Mom wanted flowers more than hamburger, but for years this simple idea apparently was privileged information for women only. I didn't know.

But we had the tracks in common, and that was huge when it came to communicating and sharing. In its own bizarre way, the intimacy we knew on those tracks was part of a synthesized romance. I think they actually kept us upright on our feet when we could have stumbled into something bad. That sounds vague because one cannot always know what disastrous possibility was avoided because they went to the right instead of to the left. I have to believe those railroad tracks were a move to the right for us.

It was more than Shell Beach, because Shell Beach is probably my fond memory alone, but I hope Mom can agree that the tracks belong to both of us.

Years later in Massachusetts I wanted to walk the tracks again with Mom, but in New England, they were used by commuter rail trains, which took away the option.

Then there was the field by the church. The football field I had painted in lime on the lot across the road. This mini football field represented only about thirty total yards, but it was enough for our purposes. We adapted touch-football rules to our area. We probably invented a few more rules that made scoring probable, but it provided me hours of pleasure with my sons. And this was during the years of the steel curtain and four Stealer Super Bowl rings!

Like the railroad tracks, this homemade football field represents more than a single event. Sometimes the simplest enjoyment, though often repeated, is lost to memory's eye, because it was blended into the mundane. Sometimes the importance of some detail of one's experience is too small to be noticed for what it really is: kissing a sleeping toddler tucked in for the night, giving a spouse a hug and kiss goodbye before starting for the day, receiving a visit to a hospital bedside, finding that someone special to you hadn't forgotten your birthday. The list is endless but it is often eclipsed by the recollection of a big event that in the scope of things has far less meaning.

It is easy for me to remember the Charismatic Conference of 1979, but it was a momentary blink in the history that is my life. However, the day-to-day moments spent with you, my sons, was that life. The football field symbolizes this. We played other games indoors and outdoors, took walks and drives to ice cream stands, even tried to do our thing with pets, two dogs and three cats, over the course of seven years, and most of these I would assume are forgotten since nothing spectacular happened along the way. But they were in themselves spectacular. They were fireworks-spectacular, because I did them with family, and nothing else I could do or think to do could possibly approach that.

I could easily find pastors who would disagree with me. They preached their allurement toward church projects, toward the success of being a preacher, not the success of being a father. It took me years to outright discredit their approach to ministry. Who was I to look at the wheat crop of their growing churches and their passion for preaching and toss it all away as so much chaff? I sought for resolution from the few clergy I held in highest regard, but none of them ever solved the problem of how much time belongs to church and how much to family.

For now, I haven't solved it either. I just gave up and have happily retreated into family, where I have longed to be all along.

Speaking of retreats, the computer games were a quiet memory. Twenty years later I would be sitting in front of the computer nursing my depression while learning to program. But now, in Burgettstown, computer games were harmless challenges. If you messed up, just start over again, which we did countless times. On a color TV set, which was by itself new to us, the games mesmerized with bright colored figures dancing around a screen at my command by control of a correctly-named joystick.

We took turns getting killed or eaten or whatever, until someone managed to escape to the next and harder level. There were a hundred levels, or so it seemed, and day after day we would make the attempt at getting to the end of them. I just want to thank my boys for the memory.

Burgettstown and computers do not go together. We were not exactly high-tech in this small community. When we ordered the Sinclair computer with its 1K of RAM, we started to leave the world of crooked railroad tracks and sulfurous basement runoff, but I didn't know it. It would be a proud idea to take credit for preparing us for our future world of information technologies, but it would be a wrong idea. I didn't see any connection. I was having fun playing games, while you, Tim, programmed—all night on occasion—on your ZX81.

Do you think God... Do you think God was... I don't know. Let's not go there for now. Isn't it interesting that sometimes what comes naturally, what feels right in your gut, seems to work out for the better in the long term? Tim, I helped you when you turned 12 and you helped me when I turned 12 in 1993. I was actually 48 going on 12 when I made my career change.

Playing in the Camp's, round swimming pool was another one of those repeated events that could fade out of sight. We would get the water circulating in one direction and drift about in a circle in the warm summer air. We created a version of water polo that worked for us to pass hours of wet fun until our hands and feet shriveled in the night air. Tim, James, you may not remember the games as such because the contests we invented where subject to personal interpretation, and polo is probably not your word for it. Maybe just "horsing around." I would often give you a ride on my shoulders in the soft waves. I trimmed down and got a little muscle definition—just a little—as a happy consequence.

The rule of thumb was that until you turned 5 years of age, I would carry you on my shoulders whether in the pool or on walks through gardens, wherever, when your little legs gave out. Little did I know that the day would come when you would carry me. Because you were there when I was at one of the lowest points in the middle to late 90's, which I must wait to relate. Because you were there, I found strength of resolve to chance an improbable career change. We actually built a relationship based on taking turns carrying one another, and I thank you now for it.

Then there was the Raccoon Creek State Park and what it symbolized. I miss the state park, with its trails for safe adventure. We were off the main road about a half mile at best, but it was as if we were lost to the world. And I had no fear of the boogie man in those woods. That was a different time and a different place, where your worst enemy was poison ivy, and Mom knew what to look for. So you guys went on ahead to scamper about and finally hide when you heard us coming.

Those woods became hour after hour of pure peacefulness. You ran ahead leaving mom and I to walk more slowly, hand in hand. I think I was beginning to get this romance thing. We were Adam and Eve, all alone and in love. It was the engagement we never really had. Romance wasn't a fireplace after all, but a woodland trail.

On one occasion mom and I took this walk without you boys. It had to be about May of 1982. I pick this date, because it was about ten months before Joshua was born. I remember thinking how Biblical it would all be if I took my Eve in my arms here in the woods and proceed on a natural course where romance inevitably leads two people in love. We didn't. We thought differently for obvious reasons, but to my mild regret, because Joshua was planned and conceived about a month later.

However you interpret things, the state park and its trails were a romantic getaway.

But Mother's day, May 9, 1983 was coming, when I would formally tell Christian Assembly goodbye, and we would also have to say good-bye to these woods and this park. I didn't realize how genuinely traumatic this was going to be for me.

A Sad Goodbye

Goodbyes are not forever.
Goodbyes are not the end.
They simply mean I'll miss you
Until we meet again!
--Author Unknown

I don't think anything is more difficult for me to relate than the two weeks in late June when I stayed behind in Burgettstown to close out this chapter of our life, while mom and you boys went north to Sharon, PA.

I think I had a reactive depression. A reactive depression, according to the textbook, is the result of grief suppressed over the loss of something or someone. A person in its grip doesn't want to die. They simply lose interest in life. It is as if a vast void has been blown in their reality, and they have no way of getting from here to there across that chasm.

I reflected back years afterward on that late June time frame and came to the conclusion that this was what I was experiencing. The pieces fit. The book's definition fit. I seemed to be mourning the loss of a congregation that I had come to love and care about.

You cannot get emotionally close to people without price. You cannot carry someone else's burden, pray for them long into the night, prepare studies and seek sermon material that would encourage them and support their passion for following the Bible, work with them in ministry, bury their loved ones, share the excitement of their good times and weep with them during the hard times, without them becoming in some way a part of what life means to you.

Yes, I think I got too close. But I didn't see this coming. I thought I was simply following Biblical example, doing what I thought pastors are suppose to do. I did it, but not with the depersonalizing mechanics of a program or clerical portfolio, not with a half-hearted empathy that vaguely understood what they were going through but losing no sleep, not with a clear sense of my own professional limitations or the limits even God would wisely place on my conduct.

I jumped in where angels fear to tread. Now here is where I was quietly falling apart. I couldn't stop weeping. I visited family after family, weeping as I went, saying goodbye to those who became a family of sorts to me. I remember driving between homes one afternoon, singing to myself as I wept what then became my favorite melody, "Jesus loves me;

this I know, for the Bible tells me so." I really needed to know this.

I had already resigned the church, so I was no longer their pastor, but I was still floating around town seeking some kind of closure, I guess. My depression denied me any right to sensible decision. I was unable to even prepare a message. On a Sunday night during this transition to my new duties in Sharon, I was invited to speak in a church in Little Washington. I had no message, so I simply opened the Bible to Genesis 1:1 and rambled for twenty minutes or so. That is a sad confession, but a real one. I couldn't wrap my intelligence around any idea, and I felt there was no one around to help me to do it. I cannot even now imagine what people were thinking about me. I didn't know at the time what I was thinking. My salvation was that my new responsibilities would start immediately in Sharon at the then CCNA, Christian Church of North America, (now, IFCA, International Fellowship of Christian Assemblies) headquarters. I depended initially on the general overseer, Rev. Saginario, to be God's tool to guide me through this transition.

I was way too close to that cliff and probably should have fallen off, though I didn't. Perhaps an unseen arm caught me.

But I know now where the cliff is and want to stay away, if ever I have future opportunity to pastor a church. Does this make the lesson worth the price? I have come to believe that caring and sensitivity with empathy are a part of ministry, and it is impossible to emotionally insulate oneself completely from what happens to such people you care about, but the minister needs to stay objective and be able to avoid the intimidating consequences of too many tears. Pastors need to carry only those burdens that in their gut they are sure are okay with God. They need to recognize what they cannot do, and what they are not chosen to do, and not to do it.

So why did I leave Burgettstown? It seems that I was simply burned out, but that wasn't it. I agreed with Mom that we needed to move on. It is not uncommon for a pastor to want to stretch his vision or revive his message in another ministry. It is not unusual for a minister to think he has done about all he can here and must move on. Today, if I had a little Burgettstown-type church, I would consider myself blessed, but then was a different time, and I still had a lot to learn.

So long, Burgettstown. May God's blessing be with you, and may you prosper in Him in all your future opportunities.

Goodbye.

The World Almanac

My life? It isn't easy to explain.
It has not been the rip-roaring spectacular I fancied it would be,
but neither have I burrowed with the gophers....
There are no monuments dedicated to me,
and my name will soon be forgotten,
but I have loved someone with all my heart and soul,
and to me, this has always been enough."
-- Nicholas Sparks

I'm in there, in the World Almanac, 1986, under Denomination, or religious organizations, and under the CCNA. That could sound impressive, if being on the Executive Board as a General Secretary / Treasurer is impressive, because that is how I made it into the book.

But we had moved to the General Headquarters of the CCNA in Sharon, PA to assume these responsibilities, more as an experiment rather than a serious career move. We lived in Georgetown, in Sharpsville, PA, and made $350 a week, which all sounds uptown from where we had come. We didn't need incense anymore.

They gave me an office which looked rather empty, almost sterile. I could sit by the hour in my cushioned chair drafting letters that needed to say difficult things to difficult people in such a friendly way that they didn't know they were being scolded. I guess it was this expertise that got me the job.

We also had two computers. One was an old Radio Shack TRS-80, and the other was an IBM with an 8-inch floppy, not exactly state of the art.

I was able to work on the organization's legal documents, as well as familiarize myself thoroughly with its theological position. I took minutes and edited them, to reflect the best board image to our constituents. The biggest thing I might have done in the sole year I was there was help organize the 1984 National Convention in Tarrytown, NY. Throw in a few business luncheons, and you get the picture. But what wasn't evident was that I wasn't happy. I wasn't being me, even though the job was nine to five, and I had more time with the family than when I pastored or taught.

Sharon was a passageway between churches, as it turned out. It was only a brief time out, to talk to Mom and catch my professional breath between ministerial races. The problem with the race was that I was sprint-ing, when it was a long distance thing. Pastors need to pace themselves and find times to restore their energy level. But I hadn't, at least not with any consistency. I was exhausted or perhaps near burning out as a pas-tor, and Sharon was my hospital bed, so I could rest awhile.

We had been in this situation before, in Canonsburg, if you recall.

A year later we would get the call to come to New England but in the meantime, I had a chance to get closer to my family. I came to realize that each one of you boys was, in fact, a lot like your dad. Each one knows a part of me although you may not be aware of this.

In brief, I have Tim's passion for discovery and problem-solving; I have Joshua's passion for ministry; and Jim and I both have a dislike for radical change. The pain of adjustment to something that wasn't me, that wasn't us, went beyond a momentary discomfort for newness. It was a painful experience from which we would eventually squirm free.

The similarities between me and my sons goes beyond this. I think they could guess a lot about me because it is true about them. They must know my weaknesses and temptations, my passions and interests.

Josh, I see me in you, not the one-year-old here in Sharon, but the young adult you would become, if I might glance ahead, when you en-tered your twenties. It would be increasingly difficult for me to object to your interests in ministry, since they were mine at your age.

Jim, when you found the new school in Sharon difficult to adjust to, was it any different than my issue with Headquarters? Not at all. Again, looking ahead, I would never look at you as somebody mysterious. For good or for bad, your interest in life and even your intellectual struggles with Bible ideas were mine, too.

Tim, I couldn't imagine a career change—again looking down time —without you and your expertise. Is it coincidence that I would go into programming also? Did I choose computer programming because it meant money, or something I could learn because I had you, or because I too had an interest in it? I guess all three, but don't minimize the third point. My interest in working with computers somehow parallels your own. Take the computer away because it is only a vehicle of interest, and we get closer to the true likeness between us, one for discovery and prob-lem-solving. I refer to program maintenance and support at work as CSI, code screw-up investigations. I love to research and find corrections and implement a better whatever. I think, Tim, you do, too.

So this little Sabbatical would be an opportunity for us as a family to take inventory of our interests and maybe get some direction for future possibilities. At the convention in Tarrytown, I was asked to lead choruses, which put me on the platform during our general overseer's message. I remember weeping behind him as he preached, because that is where I wanted to be, preaching. I wanted to be back into pastoring. He must have known this since he organized a trip for us to New England to visit the churches. I didn't know it, but he had informed the board at Norwood, MA that I would be a candidate for their pulpit.

PART TWO

Living in Massachusetts

1984   Moved to West Street in Norwood
1985   Moved to Walnut Avenue in Norwood
1986   Moved into the new parsonage that Summer.
        Purchased Astro Van
1988   Moved into Windsor Gardens (December)
        Began working at the Howard Johnson's
1989   Moved to Oak Street in Walpole
1991   Moved to Myrtle Street in Dedham
1992   Traded in the Astro Van for the Grand AM

Seagulls

Trouble is a sieve
through which we sift our acquaintances.
Those too big to pass through are our friends.
--Arlene Francis

In November of 1984, we moved to West Street in Norwood, MA. This, it turns out, was the beginning of a nine-year adventure in which we would move six more times.

I thought I had brought with us some education when it came to pastoring. I wanted to be less emotionally involved with people, so I planned to visit less. I wanted to be there as a pastor for those who needed a pastor, but visits for friendship's sake would be minimal.

I now believed that when people came to depend on you for more than what you should be responsible for as a pastor, you increase the risk of their disappointment, and therefore their anger, when you don't come through for them. Less visible means less disliked. I now wanted to focus on prayer and study and family more, but the problem I had in angering folks was more a lack of art than a lack of science. I was famous, I guess, for my availability and the people wanted to define my duties based on my benevolent approach to things.

What probably made matters go from bad to worse was a little thing called "vision," which carried an importance in New England that was not emphasized in Western PA. I eventually understood that "vision" was taken somewhat literally. It had to be some great plan organized by the pastor that the people could see. It had to be measurable by some easy comparison with other churches in the neighborhood. In fact, the only two things that meet this criteria are numerical growth and a building project, and I was not into either one of these.

My interest was somewhat diffused or blurred and not easily measured. I wanted to encourage Christian maturity through learning the Biblical message for Christians and let these Christians show their own communities what being a Christian was really all about. My thought was that God would take over from there.

I had another problem more immediate. The people in the church represented two different doctrinal positions. This conflict is known as the Calvinist-Wesleyan controversy, which has been debated for centuries, and it had infested our congregation like a incurable disease.

81

Churches have dealt with it only by taking a stand on one side or the other of the issue and inviting those of a different view to leave.

My problem was the result of my not wanting to take sides. I didn't want to go right or left, because I could not in clear conscience see the Scripture doing that. On this subject, I have never changed my mind.

While I am listing some of our difficulties up front, let me add the parsonage. The Norwood church, for the first time in its history wanted to support a full-time pastor, me, and build a house, church-owned, for us to live in. This was a challenge that required, I suspect, a degree of expertise or experience or administrative acumen that was lacking at the Norwood church. Perhaps the church board bit off more than it could chew. I know I did.

I was beginning to believe that my calling was not pastoring at all but being a forerunner. I seem to be forever going into a situation that required change, but like the marines at Normandy, the danger was greatest for the first wave.

We moved into a truly New England house on West Street. The house had narrow staircases. I had to cut the box springs of our queen-size bed into half to get it into the house. I took our den couch apart as well, and reassembled it inside.

We were hoping to move shortly into the new parsonage, but that wasn't to be. When the landlord at West Street moved a tenant into the basement, against zoning regulations and I, yes, I blew the whistle on him, we had to move or pay a rent increase that was designed to get us out. The new parsonage was not built on schedule, so we moved to Walnut Avenue first. Moving now was not like the time we packed the car with some blankets and visited Buffalo for three weeks. We had furniture. We didn't have as much as we would have after living in a brand new house, but we had furniture. This was the "before" picture. We still needed a truck but since it was still the honeymoon, the men in the church were a great help.

We were still waiting on the parsonage, so in the meantime, I thought it a good idea to organize the New England District for the religious organization we were in, the CCNA. After all, I knew the guys at the headquarters, and even though leadership had changed since I had left, it still seemed a working idea. I was not aware of a growing distance between the new general overseer and myself. I don't know if it was discontent or misunderstanding or just a leadership thing that brought him to the conclusion that he preferred another district overseer in New England to me. While living on Walnut Avenue, I would help organize the district, becoming its first overseer before relinquishing that post to another.

The title of this chapter is Seagulls? When we moved to Norwood, I was reminded of living in Buffalo. The seagulls had returned to McDonald's. There were no seagulls in Burgettstown. Seagulls also are fighters, always robbing one another of a French fry or piece of a hamburger bun. I can't say whether or not there are human seagulls in the church trying to grasp for themselves a ministry or a leadership opportunity or a microphone and fifteen minutes of fame. I think they are there, and they add to a pastor's problems, but in all honesty no names come to mind. The seagulls were a welcomed sight. It seemed a good omen since I grew up with this bird around. Time would tell.

666 Walpole Street

You will always have something NOT to worry about!
--Joyce Meyer

The church was designated by town numbering to be at 666 Walpole Street but the selectmen acquiesced and changed it to 668. True story.

Strangest thing: I always felt at home when pastoring. It seems, part of whoever I was or was becoming could only find expression here. I was told I would regret leaving the Executive Board. This was not spoken as a threat or an enticement to keep us in Sharpsville, but was the concern of an honest friend, the General Overseer at the time, who wanted me to consider carefully my move out of office.

I never regretted the move. There still is something about me that needs the pastorate to sense fulfillment. And I am beginning now in later years to figure out what it is. Josh, I guess it is a little like you and ambulances. Part of me needs to be helping someone, somehow. Part of me needs to be needed, and what better context for me when you consider my training and age than in a church full of needy people?

The difference might be that church people don't see themselves as needy. They see themselves as somehow protected by the doctrine of Grace from what ordinary people have to face. They believe that the reward for being there and being a part of whatever God is doing is God's providential care to keep them from all kinds of woes and troubles.

And yet, notwithstanding their testimony and the strength of their faith, they do have issues, and they do need pastors, or guys like me who would be pastors, to care.

The rain falls on the just and the unjust; so, even Christians need to face the reality of getting wet. They need a Biblical umbrella, if that Scriptural directive is available. Some of us are going to end up in deep water. We need to learn how to swim or at least tread water.

I have always felt there was a pulpit for me somewhere, even if I was always having difficulty finding it.

Congregations, because they are representative of people with personal problems, need pastors, and Norwood was no exception. We had a growing congregation, and like most churches, I assume, the growth represented a percentage of needy people who came there looking for quick solutions. TV preachers get people hoping for fast cures and elixirs, where one Scripture heals all. There is no such thing, but people keep hoping and thinking that tomorrow the big miracle will come and with it, instant fortune.

But tomorrow, God's solution will be to have some caring pastor ready with a realistic encouragement. Sometimes, something miraculous does happen, but one should not build a theology around it. Some things happen that go beyond coincidence and beyond explanation, and because they are good things, I have no problem crediting God. Some pastors may take partial credit, because they were there when it happened, and they may even think it had something to do with their prayer life or organizational skills, but I sincerely doubt it.

People need pastors, but, not withstanding, the Norwood church did not prove to be my home away from home. What went wrong? Something happened in Norwood for which I had documentation that I discarded in the name of forgiveness. I can be open with family here, though.

As we grew, we became a church of diverse beliefs. No heresy, mind you, but conflicting interpretations of Scriptures that, as it turned out, became the bone of contention that would eventually discipline me out of the pulpit.

I can't explain it much better, because all the dynamics of a court seem to be in play. There was denial, lots of it. There were conflicting opinions, or at least multiple opinions, that suggested a myriad of reasons for wanting me to leave. But no one actually wanted us to leave. I learned this later by a congregant, who probably to this day wonders why we did leave. Years later, there would be apologies all around, and a few hugs, but I only see this as a wish that things could have proceeded less painfully for all concerned.

Bottom line: Someone did want someone to leave the church. There may have been some who wanted me out, or maybe they just wanted people of a differing theology to leave, which they felt had come into the church because of me. Who can be sure of who's who in this battle of words that no doubt ended up injuring a few innocent folk as well.

One such issue, on the possibility of gaining and then afterward losing one's salvation, I could identify, because it was brought up in meetings. It was a doctrinal issue on which I could not take a definite stand, because I could not see it Biblically. I am reminded of C.S. Lewis's comment on the subject, in a letter dated February, 1946, "The controversy is one I can't join on either side for I think that in the real (Timeless) world it is meaningless."

My sentiments exactly. And I have had no trouble interpreting the emphasis of Scripture in alignment with this opinion.

Whether it was the last straw or the only straw, I will never know. But when stones are being hurled, people get into the fever of the thing and start throwing for any reason.

I once substitute-taught in a grammar school in Cape May. It was a fourth grade class, and most of the students were attentive. One girl stood out as exceptionally brilliant and cooperative. She sat quietly, front and center in the room, with her full attention on learning, except this one day. One of the more unruly boys began cutting up, and I failed to stop it. Before long, the class, student by student, was joining in, until at last—and to my amazement—even Miss Proper had joined the party. It took the principal to bring peace. It is a social condition that causes good people to chime in when someone starts something. It is common.

Perhaps the person who threw the first stone had a serious rationalization behind their action, but after that it is every man and woman for himself. Pick and toss. It is a favorite church pastime, according to the observations of history.

Could I have prevented it? We were in Norwood for four years, and I didn't see it coming. Honestly. I knew about the controversy, but I had been having that discussion with Christians for decades, and it had always been just a delightful disagreement. I never thought someone might turn it into a threat to ministry.

There were other issues raised as well. Some wondered what my vision was. I guess that meant that according to what they could observe, there were no favorable things happening in the church.

Some thought the offerings were not as healthy as they could be. Money seemed to be at issue.

Let's see. What else? Someone might have found out about the roll of scotch tape, Josh—you were three—you wound around my office chair. Maybe, or maybe not. Anyway, I was told to get a babysitter. Where was Mom? She had to work in order for us to have adequate medical coverage. The insurance which was eventually provided by the denomination had an expensive co-pay.

Anyway, at the time, one of my favorite characters from history was Abraham Lincoln, who even allowed his Joshua, Willy and Tad, to play in the Oval office, and that was during a civil war. I saw similarities, even if that was inappropriate of me. There would be no babysitter. Being with my boys was therapy for me, more and more. So as things got harder to deal with, I enjoyed playing with my young son and being a part of my older sons' worlds, even if all it meant was driving them to and from school or work. I also took regular walks with Mom to the public library to check out and read books on Lincoln.

I mention these tidbits of personal history because I believe that these are representative of what happens in ministry. I think today's pastors are successful because they have political savvy and have taken hold of their futures. After all, they do have the microphone and the congregation's attention. In some cases, they have invited dissidents to leave. In today's church, I think, pastors have discovered that a little take-charge attitude goes a long way to securing their interests and leadership options.

For me, this was more difficult to do, because of what I was. It genuinely pained me to have to confront someone, with a view to engineer their removal from ministry or from the church. I didn't like the idea of a fight or a debate in front of an innocent congregation who, unsuspecting, could be offended.

But you will be pleased to hear that I have since changed my mind on this subject. Sheep need shepherds to fend off wolves and put rams in their pens.

I also started up with the bonsai trees. I needed to relax. I needed to find my escapes from growing tensions. I bought hundreds of dollars worth of the little trees, and even built a cold frame at the back of the parsonage to keep them during the winter months.

These four years were not all bad, of course not. Many church services and counseling times provided me opportunity to do my pastoral thing, and I found that repeatedly meaningful.

I maintained a weekly newsletter as well that outlined my thoughts for anyone who cared to read about it. And many did.

I was visiting less than in Burgettstown, but I was indeed visiting people, and enjoying that as well. The older generation of Italians who made up the core of the faithful were the most supportive. I could include visits to them, and often eating lunch with them, among my most refreshing and memorable moments in Norwood. They were nothing short of saints, if anyone is a saint. They probably added to my reserve of strength. I would list their names if I could spell them. God has their names. That alone is necessary.

I painted a grim picture, but there were successes and good times as well. There were people who loved us and gifts at Christmas and, as I probably mentioned, a deep sense of fulfillment when my sermons and teachings were "right on." Nothing is ever all one color or all one thing. There were the good times along with the bad times.

I missed sea shells and a state forest and railroad tracks, yes. But I had bonsai and a library. And we met new friends, the Lathrops.

John and Cindy walked into the church office one day. I was at the time the district overseer. They had a passionate interest in pastoring, but no door had opened for them, and they wanted to inquire about opportunities in our district. It happened that the Newton church needed a pastor, and to shorten this account, they were candidates and accepted the pastorate at the Newton CCNA church. This was the beginning of a long and reliable friendship and, as it turned out, our roles would be reversed. Mom and I would need their friendship as once in a small way they might have needed ours. John would be with me at a future congregational meeting, called to vote us out of another church. That is another chapter.

Here, I mention the emotional support John and Cindy provided that helped us maintain our emotional balance when otherwise we might have been swept off our feet with troubles. We could have done something reckless. Eventually, part of the emotional healing process would take place at the Newton church. Mom and I attended there for months until Mom's Sunday work schedule moved us closer to home.

I owe it to you to record the final events of our ministry in the Norwood church. This is not sour grapes but a piece of personal history with which we need to be reconciled. I have said my goodbyes and am okay with what happened. Denying it or projecting blame is not an option here. So to the best of my recollection here is the short of it.

October 16, 1988, a meeting was called with district and church officers in attendance. I had received a registered letter requiring my presence, and thinking it had something to do with money, I cut a check for the district which I handed to the district treasurer just before commenting that now we can all go home. Make a mental note of my "smart" attitude. It would show up now and then when I was convinced that I had the right of way. The treasurer wasn't impressed. He told me it was more serious than that.

It turned out that some national and district officers had met the week before to discuss the agenda, and this meeting was well organized. It had little to do with money. The short of it was they had an interest in my theology regarding the possible loss of salvation --the Calvinist-Wesleyan controversy, which I mentioned already. I understood later from another national official, who was not at the October 16 meeting, that if they could have shown that my theology had changed from what it was when I became the pastor, they would have had grounds for dismissal.

I was put on a 90-day disciplinary leave of absence, which carried little to no meaning in the scheme of things, as it turned out. Ninety days later, I spoke with a church official, who told me that I had been fired. Later, he denied this. Go figure.

What happened next is the next chapter in our adventure, but what might be worth mentioning here is my meeting with CCNA officers at the motel where I took employment after I left the payroll of the Norwood church.

National and district officials met with me on December 7, 1988 at the Howard Johnson's Motel. The meeting was probably uneventful. Actually I doubt that it was worth their time, unless the executive board was simply inquiring about our departure from Norwood. The only question I recall is one of accountability. My response was that we are all accountable to each other. It is a fellowship, not a hierarchy where the person at the top has no one to police his actions --another one of my smart remarks aimed at the general overseer, to let him know that in my mind he too needed to be policed. After the meeting the general overseer sought out an audience with me in private, wondering if he had done anything to offend me. I told him there was nothing that I could think of, not knowing at the time about the meeting he had attended to draft the agenda for October the 16th.

Messy? Messy. But it did happen that way, and I would be careful finding people to blame. I know I seem to be pointing at the top CCNA leadership, but in all honesty I could not then nor now be sure of who took what responsibility. Since then, I have been reconciled with a number of principal players in this mini-drama.

For now, it was time to move on.

Today, if I could do it all over again, would I react or act in the same fashion? I would probably fight to keep my pulpit, by guaranteeing an audience with the Vice President of the organization. He was not called in, because he was not part of the plan to discipline me. If he would have advised my staying, I would have stayed.

And if I stayed, I would have taken this issue before the people. They had a right to know and—God knows—the grapevine was not silent. Certain board members would probably have been asked to leave the board. This would be difficult for me to recommend, since I have believed in the general goodness of Christians and still like the idea of forgiveness as a working principal in relationships.

I say this because I believe it is Scripturally the best approach in defense of the gospel message and the spiritual interest of the congregation.

Attacking a pastor without cause is attacking the pastorate as a principal of Biblical leadership, and it is very wrong.

They felt they had cause. I give them that.

Let's move on.

Jurassic Park

*I am in the process of starting a nonprofit organization
that gives rescued animals a home in a simulated wild environment
and, for those who have been tested on,
who are disabled, aggressive, etc.,
their own space to live out their days.*
Casey Affleck

I saw the first movie in the Jurassic Park trilogy, and I stayed fixed to
the plot until the Tyrannosaurus, the big boy, overturned the touring vehicle with the two children inside. I felt the scene was drawn out too
much. I tired of the roars and snorts that beast kept blasting through the
theater speakers. I thought it was overdone.

One summer, I had a job painting bridges for the New York State
Thruway Authority. One bridge first had to be cleared of the spider nests
found under each cross rail before painting. The first few thumb-sized
spiders were easy to splat, but after a dozen or so, the phlegm-like goo
that resulted began to sicken me. I was not a spider-killer at heart, and
this activity was making me nauseous.

Too much is too much, and I suppose that is what is becoming of our
adventure in church work. We won't have to move again, will we?

Just twice more, but I am getting ahead of myself. For now, we have
opportunity to start a new work, CCM in the Fellowship Hall of the Islington Community church on the corner of Washington and East streets
in Islington. We also held services in a side room of The United Church
of Norwood, in Norwood Center (downtown), under the old CCM ban-
ner before in my depression I gave it up. CCM stands for Christian Community Ministries, and here is how it came about.

Since I was working on a tearful depression, I was not doing much
of anything except sitting at the dining room table with packed boxes
around me wondering whatever we would do next. It was during this
time that one friend, Tom Kelley, from the Norwood church, took the initiative to find the motel job for me, based on my possible interests. I was
remembering, thinking years earlier how pleasant it would be working
an all-night audit at some hotel. This is what Gary Davis did for years,
and my own dad worked in a hotel all his adult life. Why not? All I had
to do was make the phone call and follow instructions.

The church was a different matter. A small group of people from the church had taken an interest in going with us if we stayed in ministry locally, so I went around with Tony Ferrera, who later became one of my elders and a needed support, looking for a place to hold meetings. Since I was working at the motel, it became one of the choices and the one we chose in the short term.

We held meetings initially in the Master's room at the Howard Johnson's every Sunday morning, until one day I decided to meet with the pastor of the church in Islington and ask if we could rent space in their activity room, annexed to the main sanctuary. He said, "Sure," and not long after that I filed the paperwork to get legal recognition from the IRS. We were now officially a congregation.

Tim remembers the move, no doubt, and Josh, who was ten might have some memories as well. But Jim, you had elected to stay back and let your interests run a different course. This I understood, and part of me has always stayed back with you. These were difficult days, because my choice to go or stay seemed more the necessity of circumstance than a thought through option.

1989 was the year we lived at Windsor Gardens for 1,000-plus dollars rent per month, and CCM paid that bill. Windsor Gardens to me remains a depressing place. We moved there out of necessity, not choice, since we had to leave the parsonage. It was next door and immediately available, so we gave away some of our furniture, including our refrigerator, and made the move.

I think it important to keep using the word depression, because it helps explain the context we were in. I had a new start in ministry, so it appeared, but I was not a home-missions guy, and my passion was seriously diminished in the circumstances. CCM was also in part a congregation of disowned and discouraged people. Many had their emotional and spiritual problems for which they could find no resolution elsewhere.

To be sure, many of the people who attended our church—and there were a couple hundred in total—were healthy people. They were sensitive and caring individuals who wanted to support a ministry they felt had been unjustly treated. Keep this in mind. We were not all crazy.

Unfortunately, some of the leading figures in this unusual ministry did have emotional and social problems which had gone unresolved. They brought these issues along with them. It would be like starting another relationship during a separation because the divorce is a given. The sense is that the other person is alone guilty for whatever went wrong and we are the injured party; so, another relationship is the answer.

Some of us, not just yours truly, were also pressured out of various ministries, and we gathered together to lick our wounds and get some sympathy. We lived temporarily in the euphoric excitement of a new ministry thinking things would now be different. Anybody in the know would be quick to alert us to the danger of beginning the new without reconciling with the old, but who was listening?

If I can say it with amnesty, there may even have been rams among the sheep. I discovered that the talk on the religious street and in the colleges about rams among sheep had substance. I didn't want to believe it, and frankly didn't even consider it, because in Burgettstown, no one had been seriously trying to lead the people in the opposite direction, away from the pastor. I knew a couple individuals had been unhappy with this or that, but I had seen no serious organized effort to challenge my leadership. In Burgettstown, discontents merely went home to sulk awhile. Matthew DeSantis, a missionary to Europe, once gave me sound advice while in Norwood. It would have worked in PA. "They are rocks in the stream. Flow around them!"

But this advice wouldn't have worked in Massachusetts. Rams don't decide to simply graze off to one side. They try to lead! My problem was complicated at the time, because I didn't want to believe this of God's people, and that is what I thought of church people. They call it naiveté.

This sounds terrible. No Christian would call himself a ram. No one looks at his woolly soft exterior and imagines that he also has pointed horns. I think, more to the point, he "can't help it" if other sheep want to follow him. And if he crawls under the fence into another field against the shepherd's directive, he cannot imagine the shepherd making that big of a deal out of it, since the grass over there is good. "Inevitably," he says, "the shepherd will discover that and want all of us on that side of the fence!"

What can you do with rams anyway? I don't think they make good eating. Give them to another naive shepherd, is a neat idea, but a nasty one. Best idea, leave them to God, but get them out of the fold—I mean church. I mean, your church, our church.

Lesson learned.

If there is a plus side to the inevitable dissolution of what was a promising idea, it would be the concept CCM embodied. Out of these months in Islington came a clearer and more focused interest for me. I learned more about myself and what made me tick. Out of this discovery would come a series of teachings, by the same name, the Discovery Series on Discipleship, which I would develop in our next ministry at First Baptist. Granted, this teaching didn't catch on, and every church we have attended since has had its own approach to discipleship, or whatever they want to label it. But it defined me. That was good to know.

Mill Village

Work on good prose has three steps: a musical stage when it is composed, an architectonic one when it is built, and a textile one when it is woven.
Walter Benjamin

In 1991, CCM merged legally with The First Baptist Church of Dedham, and I became an affiliated conservative baptist preacher. I appreciated this chance at jumping the theological fence and observing firsthand how another religious organization does things. Their view of Bible was a little clearer to me in some places and more vague in others, but all in all, I felt at home among them, even if they had concerns about me.

Dedham is close to Boston, and I think it is fast becoming a suburb of the city, but in the era before the civil war it was known for the textile industry and thus the early name Mill Village. So I am told. You could view Dedham in one direction as a small town, or go in another direction and get the feel of Boston. It could be the perfect location for a church which wanted to be a vital part of city missions work as well as appeal to small town folk who lived in true suburbia.

We were a merged congregation. We didn't just represent people from the city and the suburbs. We were a continuum of beliefs from pentecostal to baptist. The point is that compromises would have to be made, but Christians do not compromise beliefs, because they see this as compromising their faith. Christians go to war for what they think the Bible is saying, and here we were trying to enlist them into one fighting force, not against other Christian faiths, but against—I want to use a vague religious term here—sin.

Everybody has enough to handle with the war within: the beam in his own eye, the contradictions between what he is and what he wants to be, playacting to show himself someone other than who he really is, and what he really is thinking. How do we ever have the energy or time to attack another person? But we do.

Sad to say, people unconsciously project blame and find fault with others in an effort to sign a treaty with themselves. Somehow, winning a fight with someone else is designed to bring peace within ourselves.

It is all psychological nonsense, a need to discover that whether other people are worse off than me, theologically, morally or in any other way, is unimportant to my own emotional health issues. Proving someone else wrong or revealing their faults might take the focus off me mo-

mentarily, but sooner than I anticipate, I will find myself back on the bat-
tlefield of my own private thoughts, and the inner war will go on until I
fight it and win. This isn't as much a description of First Baptist people as
it is of church goers—no, of people in general, and maybe me in particular.

Also, I have to believe that when we merged, we introduced some
more confusion into the mix. We brought some pentecostal doctrine
along with us. On top of everything else, First Baptist was in an identity
crisis.

Perhaps I wasn't so sure about my beliefs. Am I pentecostal, or am I
not pentecostal? One baptist colleague recommended I find myself theologically before I choose a denomination. This sounds sensible, but I am
still trying to figure it all out. Now, if the pastor isn't giving clear signals,
what should we expect from parishioners?

In terms of inner conflicts, I was probably still depressed. One counselor told me it looked like a clinical depression, simply because after six
months it didn't go away.

I am going to say something here that might sound a bit judgmental,
and I apologize for that. I think some (not all) church leaders during our
stay in Mill Village had personal issues and unresolved conflicts from
previous ministries that added to the struggle that First Baptist was experiencing. The people would have gladly followed us, the leaders, if we
had a clue where we were leading them.

In addition to the doctrinal identity crisis and the personal issues
which some leadership brought with them, we were a growing church.
Others were coming out of a world of personal conflicts and were in need
of counseling. That's not a bad thing, but what was bad was our lack of
preparation to provide for this need.

They were showing up HIV-positive. They came with serious mari-
tal issues and pending divorces and an overanxious desire to jump into
new relationships. They came with unwanted pregnancies. They came
with abuse issues and overwhelming financial needs. They came with addictions that ran the gamut from alcohol to sex to gambling.

This is why we were there, to help them, but we couldn't until we
learned to work together, and an unhealthy leadership meant an unhealthy church. Inevitably we were not going to be much good to anyone. Sorry to say it.

I just painted a pretty grim picture but there was also the good side
of things. Some of the people were healthy. They were the pointing between the bricks, and without them the whole structure might have col-

lapsed. I met some baptist folk of whom I will forever be proud to speak and to whom I will be eternally grateful that they were there.

I know I run the risk of appearing hard on people whose names are absent from this list. I appear to suggest that they were not candidates for my list of saints. Some people I include with me in need of sainthood not having arrived yet. People should not be offended if in all honesty they know, as I do about myself, that they didn't deserve a hundred score on this test, at least not at the time. Others deserved the grade, and I apologize for forgetting their names. Besides, this would add pages to my story. I hope it sufficient to say "Thank you for your consistent kindness."

So our stay in Dedham was characterized by overwhelming hurt. Good people were caught in the dilemma of what to do. They reacted in a typical fashion by scrutinizing the pastor and his ministry and that was me at the time. First Baptist was in its 150th year. During that time, the average stay of a pastor was four years. I checked, and one of the longest stays was by the pastor who was there during the Civil War. He left to fight and then returned. I added his years together in my statistics.

Getting back to me, my sermons were questioned. My interest in counseling, which involved some psychology, was questioned. One elder interpreted my approach to counseling as too psychological, and psychology in his mind was not biblical. My pentecostal beliefs were becoming offensive; at least, that is how I interpreted the reaction of some very good—I keep saying this and it is true—good people. My counseling sessions got out of the confidential box, and some people felt I was advising incorrectly. Some people didn't take my counsel, and somehow I should have known that and reacted differently.

When will this tyrannosaurus go away so I can crawl out from under this wreck?

Some people began to dislike my family for one reason or another, but I don't want to go there. It simply became them against us, and that was making less and less sense to me. I only knew that moving was becoming once again inevitable. The church had taken sides. A board decision froze all new member's applications, I was told. Most of the new people that would want us to stay were not church members and couldn't vote. Voting is a very baptist thing since its church government is congregational. Some of the people, I was also told at the time, moved their offering over into special funds in order to deplete the general fund from which I received my pay. They were making a statement, as if our financial security and future somehow depended on their actions or their money. No pastor would say that. I smiled, because by that time, I was numb to it.

I must sound like a complainer, but I don't want to sound that way. I want to help us all see our own reality and not hide it under some made-up explanation or rationalization. If the church is to become the church God envisioned at Pentecost, it needs to be real, and to be real, it needs to get real, and that means facing the past.

I want to say, personally, I have no regrets for pastoring First Baptist. It was a passageway for us to our current life even if that wasn't the plan. I am glad I met the saints who attended there and to this day when people ask me about the churches I pastored, the word baptist strikes a common chord. People need to have "IFCA" explained to them, but not the word baptist. And if I meet people who are against the baptists, these people need to be clear as to what their gripe is. Many things that some find offensive are the actions of a few, who in all honesty might attend any church—not just a baptist church—and probably do.

Anyways, after leaving First Baptist and while briefly trying to hold things together in The United Church of Norwood, my depression was evident when we canceled a service and failed to tell Richard, a special-needs friend who had been with us for years. He waited outside the church for over an hour before realizing that no one was coming and returned home. It was an especially low point in my life as a pastor, but better days were on the horizon.

The good thing that came of this was a friendship with Nick and Trish Langione. They had joined the few who helped carry us along into a better tomorrow. Nick and Trish had a sensitivity and a passion that carried me through this transition to secular life. They were there to do and be what was necessary to make my dreams come true. They did want to see CCM work, and I needed friends like that at the time, even though God's wisdom, I maintain, would lead us, for the time being, away from full time ministry.

We were about ready to leave Myrtle Street for Main Street in Walpole, but before I speak of that I want to mention an Assembly of God friend whose friendship Mom and I renewed while in Dedham.

Earl

To the world you may be just one person,
but to one person you may be the world
-- Brandi Snyder

During my days at Bible School, 1965-1969, I met Earl. He, like me, was studying to eventually become a pastor, and together with Sandy his wife and their son and daughter would unfortunately experience some of the traumas we knew.

In 1990, living in Dedham, Mom and I renewed old friendships and made a trip to Vermont to see them. I was reminded of pleasanter times as we reminisced. When Earl died of cancer in 2005 we attended the services to say a final goodbye for now to an old friend.

I mention Earl even though he was not directly connected with our years of going from here to there because through the years I would be reminded of his gentle spirit and his pastor-like sensitivity. Earl could read the heart. Earl was capable of knowing what you meant to say but couldn't, what was important to you even if you had no occasion to share such deep thoughts. And beyond this, Earl could say something to you in passing which was so spontaneous and natural for him that he couldn't recall saying it, although you built a life on his encouraging words.

When the church suggested that it didn't want me, I could understand, but when it let him go, in my mind, it sold its spiritual birthright for a bowl of the man-made pottage.

It was in our freshman year at NBI, if I remember correctly, that Earl and I were part of a team of students sent to Williamsport, PA to canvas the neighborhood for a local A of G church. We spent the night in a small trailer set off from a main house belonging to a family in the church. The trailer was in a wooded area nestled among the trees down a small path about 30 yards away from the house. The house must have been built to order with an open grill or barbecue pit, stainless steel, in the middle of a huge, modern kitchen. That was all I recall seeing of the house, but the spacious beauty of the place was clearly visible, and the comparison was brought out in greater contrast with the little trailer which Earl and I were given for sleeping quarters. It had one room, nearly wall to wall mattress, probably queen-size, which Earl and I had to share. The girls on the team got the house. That's just how we did things back then.

Before turning in for the night, Earl turned to me and remarked,

"Not everyone could camp out like this, John. You have what it takes to go wherever God asks you to go."

Who knew that I would want to hang a career on that kind thought. Earl didn't know that I was just the opposite. I spent twenty years in the same house on Herkimer Street in Buffalo with only an occasional and nostalgic filled overnighter now and then. This trailer was not my kind of experience, but Earl complimented me on my potential to endure any-thing for God and he placed me in that compliment as one among many. No one had done that before. My level of self-respect was near the bot-tom of things, and Earl just brought it way up with one kind word.

How could this be true? Well, that requires my telling you some-thing I have told no one. I am not sure even your mother knows. It has to do with childhood woes, not abuse, but physical problems that I faced that kept me out of social circles in school, not being able to join in dodge ball while in grammar school. This may seem insignificant, and maybe it is, but I'll explain in a minute how it happened and how it meant that I never learned a level of confidence that gives a kid a sense of achieve-ment that spells self-respect in adult life.

Years later I would recall this trailer incident, and often—I might add—to bolster the courage to go through one more "overnighter in a trailer" episode in life.

Earl could handle the small trailer. Earl was to me this ideal. He was the ideal dresser, which included his curly red hair perfectly brushed. He was the ideal friend, since he was capable of such sensitivity without prejudice, and I could go to him and latch on to him as a friend when I needed one. And most of all, he would make the ideal pastor, not only because he genuinely cared about people but he could endure with a smile anything life tossed at him.

This would prove itself true when in his fifties he was diagnosed with cancer which became God's vehicle to call him home to Glory. I had to say it that way because I believe it! I believe in God's love and I knew that Earl lacked no faith required for providence to stay in control of things. In addition, Earl was my forerunner. It seemed that if I went through it, he was first. It was symbolic that we shared a night in a trail-er. Truth be told, he was first to open the trailer door and go in.

Mom and I visited Sandy and him when trouble was once again brewing for us, this time in Dedham. Troubles? Earl had been there. He and Sandy knew what we were facing, and it was good to call him friend.

It was not hard to think of him when I too was, years later, diag-nosed with cancer.

102

Living in Massachusetts

What's this childhood trauma that made Earl's compliment so all fired important to me? I know you know I grew up with asthma and all the "itises" that come with it: bronchitis, bronchial pneumonia, double pneumonia, whatever. I spent weeks at a time in bed covered with heated cloth diapers and Vick's vapor rub, but you knew this, too. What you didn't know was what life was like for me during the twelve years of my life between ages three and fifteen. In 1965 everything changed for the better but even today, fifty years out, the memories are vivid.

Grandma tells me that old Doc Quinn, our family doctor, made a medical blunder that did a number on my metabolic system. I needed penicillin for a fever and grandma told the doc on the phone that it was for John Henry—me—but the doc heard the Henry part only—Grandpa. I at age three was given an adult dosage of the stuff, which messed me up, according to the story. Whether I got the story straight or whether Grandma had it straight I don't know. It seemed at the time a plausible explanation, but what do I know. We are old-school Germans and are capable of telling convincing stories based on the unbelievable.

What I do know is that for a dozen years my life was characterized by relative inactivity when it came to school and especially physical education. What I am attempting to relate is the social isolation I experienced while growing up that never helps one's self-esteem. I remember church picnics were basically an occasion to sit quietly on some piece of playground apparatus and pass the time drawing circles in the dust with a stick until it was time to go home.

Along with poor social development came a sense of Mia Culpa. It was easy to fall into this frame of mind since I was having trouble placing any serious importance on my contribution to others. I couldn't see any value in what I provided. It would have been different if, say, in a game of dodge ball I had been able to eliminate a few opponents and contribute to a win. Such competition seems like an incidental thing, but in youthful development it can play a very important role.

Anyways, if anyone wanted to fault me for something, which memory reminds me was frequent in play, I accepted blame and put less and less value on my own contribution to things.

Dreams require self-esteem. A person needs to know their potential for accomplishing something in life and have a growing sense of its possibility. Going through life blaming oneself for what goes awry, thinking it has to be "my" fault, considering other peoples' opinions and advice always better than one's own, is not a good idea if you want to be someone or do something with your life. It is called intimidation, and it bumps you right out of any leadership role. Now, your own future requires your ability to decide for yourself if you want to arrive there safely and emotionally intact.

You see what this all had to do with Earl? For the first time in my recollection, someone gave me permission to be me. Someone thought it was a good idea. Someone thought I was capable of being something, even if it posed a challenge. Someone, Earl, thought I was up to the task of whatever ministry I choose to go into.

Earl said all of that in one comment that to him was a passing thought, but to me, the little boy who couldn't play dodge ball, it was an awakening.

I didn't learn all this at the time, and certainly my esteem issues continued to follow me and no doubt hurt my chances to pastor churches.

I have also viewed life as a contest of sorts. I wanted and continue to want to be the best at something. I still seem to have a need to play dodge ball and win, to know that I can be someone. I need to be the little engine that could. I have had a need to be an expert at something.

Now, all of this is an emotional overdose. It is okay to be among the best or—better yet—it is okay to be okay with one's own potentials and accomplishments, to see these clearly for what they are and take only the credit due. That's the ultimate lesson for me that Earl brought to my attention.

I remember Earl.

PART THREE
Out of Ministry

1993 Moved to Main Street in Walpole
1995 Returned to College, Framingham State
1998 Graduated in May with BS in Computer Science
1999 Purchased the Toyota Camry
2002 Moved to Foxboro (June)
2005 Moved out of Foxboro
   Purchased the Toyota Matrix
2007 Purchased the Subaru Legacy

Young Again

Out of 10,000 feet of fall, always remember that the last half inch hurts the most. — Captain Charles W. Purcell, 1932

So that was that. And what was that all about? From 1969 to 1993, actually, 24-plus years, 7 ministries, and 5 churches later. There were broken relationships and also some serious reconciliations. I look back and note the major characters of each ministry, which (with the exception of Burgettstown, where we left on our own) found me short of a promise or lacking necessary requirements for their commitment to whatever I was offering. These major characters, one by one, eventually met with Mom and me, took us out to lunch, or hugged us tearfully, or simply made the trip, maybe hundreds of miles, to see us to seek a reconciliation.

As I mentioned, I was primarily a teacher and not an administrator. Everyone saw this. As a counselor, I liked to let people talk, and I'd listen. As a pastor, I wanted people to trust in self-expression, and I wanted the boards to own their decisions. I was the dye in the live tissue—if I may—that would expose the condition for good or bad.

But that was before. Now, it was time for a career change, time to return to college and try to make a life and a living, doing something else.

You already know the story, because I have related it a hundred times at each family get-together, of when I stood in line to register for college. I was entering Framingham State College, and I just turned fifty. That seems young to me now, but not at the time. When I reached the registrar's table, a young adult, probably in his early twenties, stared up at me in wonderment and asked, "Are you a student?"

Yes I was, and not the continuing-ed kind. I enrolled in day school to be counted among students who were my sons' ages, maybe younger. I was young again. Hanging around young adults has a positive effect on one's interest in life. I was recharging and planning a second career, something a few men my age have found difficult to do.

In Buffalo, 1964, a gentleman then in the church I attended had lost his job and was attending the State University of New York, to become a lab assistant in chemistry. He was struggling, understandably, with organic chem, and since I was also at SUNY at the time and majoring in chemistry, I consented to help him.

I thought of him when now it was my turn to go back to school. I needed to take steps to make it work. What drove me was a common academic interest with you,Tim. I needed to know also that I had a tutor better than the one my friend had in 1964.

My plan was—and I worked this plan—to take one class the first semester, and if that worked out, I would take two the second and then go full time.

I also needed to play politics. I was no longer in my twenties, and this time I had to pass the course so I was quick to ask questions in class. If I didn't understand something, much to the joy of the other students, I spoke up. When a twenty year old doesn't get it, they sit silently, probably hoping he will get his answers later from the text. It doesn't work that way. I, however, discovered that professors like questions, and I endeared myself to a few of them. One professor actually paid twenty-five cents for every correction a student found in the text book he wrote. I earned a little money.

I got the flu one semester and missed an important assignment given by another instructor. With one day left to complete it, writing some machine-language code, I tossed some letters on a page and flunked the quiz. My fellow students thought it unfair and went to bat for me hoping the instructor would give me another chance.

He didn't; so it was then I knew that I had to play the school game with him a little differently. When he handed out projects and told the class we would work two people on each project, I knew I needed to pair up with the smartest and most teacher-liked student. If I was going to get a D, so would the teacher's pet. We both got an A.

My most memorable experience was in lab on a Saturday, getting my project ready for review. I was paired on this project with a young lad who was probably nineteen, if that. I chose him to make his lab experience a little more pleasant, since I felt by this time I knew what I was doing and wanted to do, and I thought this would make it easier on him. I know, I am a nice guy.

The project I chose was to build a circuit with wires and computer chips that could simulate Booth's algorithm for multiplying and dividing. (Booth's approach has also been called "Arabian math" and is just a way to multiply and divide using binary math.) I had in front me a computer perforated board with computer chips and wires all over the place.

My partner went into the lab on a Friday without my knowledge and rearranged the wires to make things look neater and the connections easier to view. This is a good idea, but he got one wrong.

When I came in Saturday, the following day, the board looked good but it didn't work when I tested it. It couldn't even multiply two times two. And I didn't have a clue why. How was I going to test hundreds of connections with a voltmeter this late in the game? My anxiety kicked in big time and what made matters worse, I needed new glasses. I needed to bend over the board with a magnifying glass a few inches away just to check connections.

Get the picture, and do you understand my panic? This project was our course grade. I cannot find the words to explain how I felt at that moment. I stepped back and yelled, "No! No!" I kept saying it shaking, clinching my fists, wondering how I could reach my partner whose phone number I did not have. And besides, it was too late. Monday was D-day (due day). On an anxiety scale of one to ten, ten being the day (years later) that the doctor told me I had cancer, this was about a nine.

The only time really that my anxiety was off the scale was the day my granddaughter Kayda was born, more than 10 weeks early. I couldn't measure that level of worry, concern, and frightful sadness that was about to overwhelm me. And when that little girl made it, my level of excitement and joy was just as high.

But here in the lab I was beside myself because this crazy circuit was that important to me. I had spent all semester on it. What else can I say?

I prayed. I stepped back and begged God to show me what was wrong with it. Then I leaned forward and—no kidding—began to stare at this orange wire near the bottom center of the board. I grabbed my magnifying glass and took a closer look and then almost as if on a hunch or a gut feeling I moved one end of the wire to another terminal.

It worked! I took the voltmeter and measured the voltage drop across where it is and where it was and sure enough that was the error. My partner had gotten this one connection off by one terminal. See it any way you want but I am persuaded that God was in someway there and He directed me.

I graduated summa cum laude, which had no value, it turned out, in my ability to work in industry. Companies wanted real experience, which I had gotten programming at the motel. What a 3.78 GPA gave me was confidence and a sense of achievement, which by now you must realize is important to me.

I went home after graduation and did nothing, though. I was discouraged, because I was thinking of taking my experience writing toy programs into the real world. I was going to pretend to be a programmer, something I knew absolutely nothing about. Depression is depression. Thanks, however, goes to you, Jim, and your bride Angela, who wrote my resume and put it out on the network. One day I got a call from a hi-tech recruiter in Burlington. He introduced me to MFS in Boston, and on July 27, 1998, I began working as a programmer-analyst for a company that has proven to be a financial life saver.

Truth be told, this period in my life was not characterized by careful planning and forethought. I was winging it, following the river of my feelings and opportunities as they came. I told Mom often that I felt like I was jumping out of a plane and hoping the parachute opened, because if it didn't... All our future would hang on the choices we made in 1993-1995. All our money and a large chunk of debt we had dumped into the possibilities that returning to school might offer, and I only hoped that it wasn't a black hole.

I was quite down in the dumps, and in that frame of mind, people generally do not plan their futures. I wasn't excited abut returning to college. I was apprehensive, to say the least.

I did enjoy programming but more as an escape from reality than a passageway into it. Ever since the middle 80's and the Sinclair, I had found the simplest computer operation fascinating. I actually found it exciting to type in "2+2" in some computer language and watch the output come up "4." If I had played and won the lottery I would have played with the machine just for the fun of it, to watch it print out "2+2=4."

The parachute opened.

Grandma's Homemade Chicken Soup

Kind words, kind looks, kind acts and warm handshakes,
these are means of grace
when men in trouble are fighting their unseen battles.
-- John Hall

Since I left Buffalo for school, I have been in at least 12 different churches over 40 years. That's a new church, on average, every three or so years. Our longest stay in any one ministry was seven years.

I have now been at MFS Investment Management for about 10 years, my longest stay anywhere. What is the secret of longevity?

I found out I like discovering solutions for problems, or in developer's terms, bug-fixes. I am a CSI agent, Code Screw-up Investigator. In the pastorate, the idea of interest was helping people, solving some of their spiritual or emotional problems, which I guess is far more difficult and involved.

I discovered that MFS management, although there is some degree of politics nevertheless treated people with a considerable degree of equality. Maybe they needed to do this to avoid lawsuits. Even so, I never felt like a second-degree citizen. I never felt put down, even though I brought the fear of such along with me. Programmers review code; they don't review each other.

In the church over the years, we took personal blame for many broken things needing to be fixed. Somehow, it was important to assign blame, although why will never be clear to me. A couple separated, a marriage on the rocks, an unruly child, the absence of some gift in the church, the shortage of funds, all needed a pastor's expertise.

Respect is another matter. At MFS some of the developers see me as a guru or expert. I have often been called in as a consultant to address a computer issue, even if I didn't think I was the man for the job. This taught me to build bridges to people who did know what to do.

I lost the church's respect, and when I saw it happening, I couldn't find the way to stop it from happening. The only thing I can think of is that the church expects its pastor to be a top-notch administrator and fund-raiser, and that simply isn't me. Also, today's pastor is part dictator and part benevolent leader, that is, a benevolent dictator. There isn't enough dictator in my psychological make-up, sad to say.

There is something else about the current leadership, or management, at MFS. When I was out on disability for four weeks during my two thyroid operations, I received two get-well packages, one from the entire department, no doubt directed by management, and another personally from the Chief Operations Officer. The COO sent me a box of Grandma's Chicken Soup with a big bowl (sent via a website) instead of flowers, along with a friendly reminder of how much I was missed at work. I was overwhelmed with such thoughtfulness. I wrote her in an email:

I unwrapped your gift just moments ago, and want to hurry off to you a thank you.

Your gift of Grandma's Chicken Soup is to me far more than a kind gesture or thoughtful expression during my recovery.

It is all of this and more so. It symbolizes the kindness and the general working atmosphere that makes MFS Investment Management a great place to work. And it shows that this thoughtfulness, this caring, and the kindness that comes from it start at the top.

I was unprepared for your gift. I am overwhelmed, simply because in all my travels and all the leaders over the years I have met and worked with and worked for, there have been none to approach this level of concerned awareness. You have passed the finish line while others have not left the starting gate.

You need to know that while convalescing, I have been working on my memoirs and have been reminiscing over the many stormy seas my wife and our sons and I traversed before we found the MFS haven. The chapter on MFS should be called Grandma's Chicken Soup? I like it!

I had emailed some district officials I know in religious organizations, but did not hear back from them. I am not complaining. I am underscoring the MFS relationship.

MFS also pays me. This sounds obvious, but when it was discovered that the industry was offering developers 12% more than I was making at the time, MFS gave me a 12% pay raise. Granted, their effort is directed at making my job position competitive, but regardless of the reason behind their generosity, they provided my family and me with two college educations, a retirement fund which is well on the way, and monthly payments on our own home. MFS takes no vow of poverty, nor expects anyone working there to do such. I have also received yearly bonuses, which have continued to date.

When I was pastoring, October was pastor-appreciation month, when pastors received gifts and offerings in appreciation for their service and ministry. I was never so honored. Just pointing out a difference.

We have our stressful moments at MFS, but they are interspersed with laughter and Nerf-ball tossing. Meetings at MFS are generally times of sharing the latest comical situation before discussing business. More often than not, a decision is the result of 99% vote in favor, and even when management overrules, we tend to accept it. We might have walked away grumbling, but somehow realizing that, had we been where management sat, the decision would have been the same.

In spite of all this, I still would favor pastoring if I could, but not as an administrator, only as a teacher. I would leave MFS with undying appreciation for what they did to make my future possibilities my realities.

Finally

The task of self-knowledge and of further self-development is
of such importance and seriousness...
that to attempt it any old way... is impossible.
The person who undertakes this task must put it first in his life... --George
Gurdjieff

After all is said, I begin to see myself either as a failure or someone who went into the wrong profession, but I maintain neither is true. I was going to call this chapter "Self-praise" or "Self-justification," but both of these phrases suggest something else to discuss about the lack of humility, or a need to admit wrong. I don't want to go there. I want to simply see the positive side of things.

There is a positive side.

Because I was a teacher at heart, I naturally encouraged people in the church to develop, to develop their ideas, their interests, and their ministries. Over the years, many honored this privilege and discovered their talents within church ministry, but some used this approach as an opportunity to take charge of things, over my pastoral leadership. In the pecking order, so to speak, I was by choice near the bottom of the line, hoping not to get pecked.

I got pecked. Nevertheless, I saw those who were being fulfilled in meaningful ways helping others, and I was encouraged. I didn't want to become defensive and put a stop to individuality. Sounds archaic, but I know of no better way to say it. People need people. We need each other, and need is the operative term. This is not immediately apparent to the many in the church who have sat quietly by and let the few do everything that has to be done. Nor it is like me to replace genuine self-discovery with a questionnaire and application form.

The church, too, over the years has turned most opportunities for ministry into ritual and even mechanical or programmed responses. A good example would be collecting the offering. When taking money from people heads the list of things to do for God, I think we are off track. So I made a stab at getting people involved with people. Give them a chance to take the puzzle piece of their own personality and complete the picture of Christian community.

Well, it didn't seem to work, but I have another operative word here: seem. Mom and I were in effect joining countless other pastors and their spouses across the country, all pioneering an idea. We were not alone, although we may have thought we were. We were the first wave of marines to hit the beaches. We were hacking our way through the jungle of old overgrown ideas that served an earlier time in church history but now blocked the path to where, I maintain, God wanted to take His church next. We need to ask ourselves if the churches we had pastored would be where they are, speaking of their success, had they never met people like us. Would their current pastors be prepared to administer in the atmosphere that we found when we had arrived?

Today's pastor is better able to administrate in an atmosphere of general acceptance to their leadership, for one. Some might conclude that it is the person in the pulpit that commands that level of respect, that it has nothing to do with past ministries. That is not my view. I believe people learn from their past relationships, and they carry those lessons forward to the present.

Some of yesterday's pioneers were specialists. They were in town to take a congregation to a new place in its history. Some pastors were there to bring a church through its first building projects. Some became a church's first full-time pastor. Some oversaw a church's personality going from upper-middle-class society to inner-city mission or the reverse. Some churches simply struggle with the idea of growth, because more people means more responsibility and more cooperation and, at the same time, less power.

What I am saying is that I think we made a difference wherever we went. Burgettstown might have been the only ministry that didn't challenge my specialty. It was the only one that embraced it. Perhaps that made it a time to develop the talents or abilities I would later use elsewhere. What about the other churches I pastored?

West Cape May was a humble beginning, but we made a difference there by raising the equity of a piece of property later used as the downpayment on a beautiful new edifice in Cold Springs. This is a small but real something.

The year we spent at the headquarters was significant, not only because of my ability to be nice to people, but also because the then-CCNA was seeking to revamp their image to include the non-Italian. They wanted a little German-Irish mix thrown in, so they invited me to serve on the Executive Board. I think that was historically significant for the organization, a step toward a level of unity that opened the door to a multi-cultured church.

Norwood, for the first time in its short history, wanted a full-time pastor and wanted to mortgage a parsonage for him to live in. Someone needed to play the pastoral role for this experiment in financial firsts, I guess. I would not have chosen me, but we were there when it happened, and that was four years another pastor did not need to experience.

The biggest something to me was our stay at First Baptist. This church was attempting a merger between two different groups who were theologically worlds apart. This kind of unity is happening today, but I maintain that the invitation to such an idea is at first difficult to accept. It is an idea that needs to grow on a church. We more or less shocked them culturally with an idea I believe would become the future for many congregations.

In general, I want to believe that church congregations, too, have growing pains, and someone has to parent them through them.

Now What!

When all else is lost, the future still remains.
--Christine Bovee

Jesus' final words on the cross were (actually only one word in Greek), "It is finished." These words have meaning to me perhaps in an uncommon way. Let's look at it only from a literary perspective and not a theological one. The single word in Biblical Greek was written in the perfect tense which signified three things.

In the language of this single word, Jesus' work as finished was decisively done, completed at last. He will never have to come here again. Tomorrow, He could go on with something else.

Secondly, His life's work—or for us, life's ambition—was seen as totally done, with nothing left to do, nothing left undone, all loose ends tied up, all details tended to. In retrospection, in His mind, He did not forget or fail at any part of His life's mission, His raison d'être was fulfilled. Many have opportunity to reach such a conclusion at life's end, so this need not be above our own possibilities.

Thirdly, His life's work was viewed at that moment as done. The moment had come, finally come. If His life's work was done, this moment could be tied to His death in peaceful resignation. With His mission complete, He could breathe His last breath without regret or irreconcilable sadness. There is no change-of-life panic here. Death was not a frightening prospect in life, but a necessary part of it. As strange as that sounds, it has validity for anyone who comes to the end of their days and can say that the things they wanted to accomplish and the places they wanted to visit they have. This is a great frame of mind to have when you reach your 80's.

We know what His death means to Christianity, but I am viewing this moment from His personal perspective not ours. It might be a bold thought but—go with me here—after walking from one end of Palestine to the other and back again for two-plus years, weary and exhausted, He finally could exit this world satisfied that He had fulfilled what He came to do.

I would like that to be my experience. But what is my calling? You might ask this, since no door opened to me to continue my education and teach on the seminary level. I was not able to nor did I see fit to knock a door or two in to necessitate my success in ministry. I pastored passively, but I did it by design or intentionally. I always hoped that given the chance, Christians would be able to do the right thing, if they knew what the right thing was. I wouldn't have to demand it. Fact remains that church leadership and I never did get along, and in all innocent candor I cannot be sure I ever knew why. But one guess I have is that I was not demanding enough. My counseling was indirect; my teaching was open to discussion; my brand of pastoring was benevolent.

So here I am working a secular job, riding a commuter train to work while scribbling down this thoughtful question.

What is my life's mission? Like Jesus, I would like to know what it is and that I completed it when in fact I have completed it. I have my thoughts on this topic. My wife, my sons, my family are a key part of them.

This reminds me of my favorite hymn. I hope you don't think your dear old Dad a kook, but I want to tell you how it happened that "Amazing Grace" by John Newton became my favorite hymn. It was 1960, and church camp had just ended. I hitched a ride for the return trip home in the back seat of a 1959 Chevy Impala, driven by the mother of one of the campers. Her daughter sat beside her with, if memory serves, another friend.

Here is the kooky part. As I usually do, I was enjoying my backseat window view, when I found myself hearing a chorus of Amazing Grace. Now, the understandable assumption is that the singers were the ladies in the front seat. I grant you that, and maybe so, but the music was crystal clear, the harmony, perfect, and I could hardly believe my ears at how full the music sounded, as if more than three persons were singing it. Also, it was summer, with the car windows rolled down as we sped along on the New York State Thruway toward Buffalo. The music I was hearing had no accompanying rush of air or road noise. It was as if I was wearing Bose noise-canceling headphones, but even clearer.

About thirty seconds in, or one stanza, I guess, the music stopped, and all I could hear was the hum of the tires against the road. I focused on the women now who were talking. I do not remember their conversation or even if I could make it out. Nonetheless, the noise filter was now off, as a heard them talking with all the surrounding noise of tires humming and trucks swishing by.

Who was doing the singing? How was this simple song in my head? If the women were my choir, they totally missed their calling. So not answering the question who, I needed to focus on the what, or the words. They were genuinely inspired and inspiring to me.

Out of Ministry

Years later I would reflect on one of Newton's stanzas, which sums up what I think now:

> *Through many dangers, toils and snares,*
> *we have already come.*
> *T'was Grace that brought us safe thus far,*
> *and Grace will lead us home.*

PART FOUR

Pastoring: What have I learned?

What have I learned in all of this? Can I see the then and the now as two different parts of one life? They are linked. They are points A and B and are connected, but they are not the same point. Can I get from A to B?

The past was riddled with bad decisions, missed opportunities, hurtful relationships, angry words I cannot take back, and mistakes in judgment and action, but this wasn't all there was to it. It helped me see who I was and where my concerns lay. I tried to be someone I was not. I tried to administrate churches when I wanted to teach Christians. I tried to raise money and organize picnics and skating parties, when nothing could possibly be further from my real interests. I often tried to help individuals when I didn't have a clue what was wrong with them. I only knew that someone had to do something, and I was their pastor. This was a mistake. I spent too much time with people not my family. I took a vow of poverty, in essence, which was not in the best interest of the people who were my life, my family. I lived with the depressing thought that I am inferior. This was also wrong. I am the best at being me, and me is what the people I care about need.

I must warn you, I get a little preachy.

I'm One of the Best

We must all hang together, or assuredly we shall all hang separately
— Benjamin Franklin

Christian unity is a big matter to me. Disunity among Christians is a thorn in the flesh for every Christian.

President John Adams, whose father was a deacon of puritan persuasion, wrote in his diary about "ecclesiastical councils" and what David McCullough called "the kind of contention that could surround a preacher."

Adams commented, "I saw such a spirit of dogmatism and bigotry in clergy and laity, that if I should be a priest I must take my side, and pronounce as positively as any of them, or never get a parish, or getting it must soon leave it."

McCullough affirmed that Adams had not the "heart" for it—we might say the stomach—and knowing innately that his dad would understand, Adams became a lawyer instead.

Doctrinal differences are a challenge to unity. Ministers built ministries around collective beliefs that would distinguish them from other Christian groups. Originally this was probably a good idea, because it was probably a God idea. We recognized that at different times in the history of the Christian church, an emphasis was needed on one part or another of the Christian message.

Christians, perhaps because they are human, tend to like some part of this message better than others, so, they decide to make that one particular part their trumpet call over other parts that might be equally important. I imagine that this is how Protestantism came about. Maybe this is how the denomination was invented. It is as if each denomination had a piece to the same puzzle. Each one had a specific message for people, something important to offer. We are a bit naive within Christianity to imagine our denomination as the only true church. History does confirm our need of one another across these doctrinal boundaries.

It seemed to Martin Luther, the Reformer of the 16th century, that the church needed to talk more about faith and less about penance. He came to conclude that if Christians lived by simply trusting God for their salvation, some of the things Christians were then doing to get on God's good side, like penance, it would be clear, were overdone or overemphasized. The faith-penance continuum is one of many which Christians find

127

themselves trying to understand. When we swing too far one way or the other, we remove a very important part of the overall message.

Well, it seems that once Martin Luther broke free, a new denomination, The Lutheran Church, was started, which I am given to understand was never his intention. Nonetheless, it became an easy thing to start other Christian religious groups, the Anabaptists in Europe and the Presbyterians in England. And everyone knows how Henry VIII argued for the birth of the Church of England, and eventually the Episcopalians came into being. The Pentecostals showed up around 1900.

Before one credentialing board, I was told—and it sounded so logical and so right at the time—that the "church's" beliefs must be clarified in the weekly pulpit, or else God's people may lose sight of how important these beliefs really are. They knew I didn't agree, so they called me vague and denied me credentials, at the time. I would eventually get those credentials, later, before a different committee. In the meantime, I understood their concern. The unspoken sentiment is that in lieu of God's ability and dedication to protect His message and His church, we need to defend it. My problem remains that I cannot imagine God allowing His church—and therefore His message—to fade away into meaninglessness. And if He does, who are we to stop it from happening? Anyways, I don't want to believe in a God I cannot trust, whose passion for His own message has died, or who is powerless to prevent its extinction.

It is the poem of "The Hammer and The Anvil" by John Clifford:

Last eve I passed a blacksmith's door
And heard the anvil ring the vesper chime;
When looking in, I saw upon the floor,
Old hammers worn with beating years of time.
"How many anvils have you had," said I,
"To wear and batter all these hammers so?'"
"Just one," said he, then said with twinkling eye,
"The anvil wears the hammers out you know.'"
And so, I thought, the anvil of God's word
For ages skeptics blows have beat upon;
Yet, though the noise of falling blows was heard,
The anvil is unharmed — the hammers gone!

I don't think any single church or denomination could be able to promote the entire message of Bible truth, because it would take more sermons than you could preach in 52 Sundays a year. Besides, the people sitting there could be easily confused, because they would be asked to process all the truth in the Bible at once, and that would be a superhuman task. Each denomination could rightfully claim a piece of the truth. They did this not so much because they thought no other church has anything to offer (although some might think so), but they felt that they didn't preach it, no one would, and that truth would be lost.

But preachers generally had a rough time with the idea that someone could be better served in another church other than theirs. It was the same for the kind of worship or ceremony offered on a Sunday morning as it was for the doctrine. They wanted you to try their brand, because they thought it was most conducive to what allowed God to do His thing. Some of my generation still wonders how a Christian could ever prefer what goes on in the church down the street over what God is doing here.

There is something very wrong with this view of things, but whatever is wrong with it may not be immediately evident to my generation of preachers. Even if we were aware, how could we change it? It would take God, and what He might do would have to set a precedent.

Historically, the church has been dividing, not merging, over the past two millennia. I think God had to know this all along, and He had His timetable for making a move to unite His people. Still, my generation could not find the way to start such a change to unite our differences and bring Christianity back to its humble beginnings. Sadly, it seems the church was in one accord at its birth, but not since. On ecumenical differences, C.S. Lewis wrote in May 1939, "A united Christendom... I confess I cannot see." Pastor Snook maintained that there would never be only one denomination and I agree. For total unity, denominationalism has to disappear.

But I must confess, son, that I never could support disunion, ever since I understood that the word used for division in Paul's letter to the Galatians, which Paul held up as a no-no for Christians, means "differing schools of thought," i.e., denominations. It is so easy to find Bible writers pleading for unity, even to the point of recognizing it as an essential part of ministry.

I began to see the differences, however, as important, but only as an essential part of one's private faith. Convictions are a vital part of everyone's life, and people cannot ignore conscience and principal and expect to be healthy and happy. That is true of everyone. Christians need to have a view or understanding of Scripture, in a way that encourages them to do what they believe is right for them. A clear understanding of Biblical principles boosts enthusiasm for living. I like to say that the Bible is a pharmacy of many thoughts, none of which are universal elixirs.

Truth is truth, but how it applies to someone's life requires wisdom. Pastors need to know how to dispense these truths in a way such that it applies to the lives of his listeners, and that ain't easy.

TV preachers have no clue how to pull this off. TV preachers are not made of the stuff pastors are made of. They are simply TV personalities. I think they should stick to basics or, in other words, evangelism. In that way, Billy Graham was always right on.

There are some pastors whose passion to help people exceeds the four walls of their churches, and they need a larger public. I think they genuinely care for the people in the community where they live. The example that comes to mind is Pastor Van Riper. Even retired from the church, he continues to maintain a radio broadcast accepting prayer requests on the air. I think he is for real.

Truth is truth. And since truth is absolute—like math—it seems I just spoke heresy when I said its meaning is relative to the individual living it. How can there be more than one meaning behind an absolute idea? There can't be, but there can be more than one application. Biblical truth is Biblical principle, and how these are to be applied is as individual as our needs. Does this make any sense?

I enjoyed being in Burgettstown, even though it was a humble ministry. I had a chance there to dialog and fellowship with charismatic Catholics. I had opportunity to work with Presbyterians. I involved myself with the church across the creek while they were between pastors. I visited their sick, married their youth, and buried those who preceded us to God.

It was not without its price, I guess. Not because people were confused about where I stood doctrinally. That issue would not come up until we moved to Massachusetts. No, the people of Burgettstown were more community-oriented. Their difficulty with me was a need for more individual attention, and I must have been spreading myself too thinly.

Unity has to deal as well with the independent spirit of the clergy. Ministers also like to complicate things and I think this is done in an effort to show the world that they know something other clergy don't, or are qualified to do something others are not. I won't bore you with the philosophies we studied and the theologies we drafted, which were so mentally involved as to require a college degree to discuss them.

Churchgoers know nothing about this, although they think they do. Truth be told, they sing songs that contradict what they think they believe, and I have discovered that much of their understanding is nothing more than rote catechism. God love them, they simply parrot what someone in a pulpit or a book told them to say. In my opinion, this is where religious clichés come from.

I didn't attend seminary. It was not a possibility for me, much to my regret. Maybe this means that I don't really know what I am talking about.

And maybe not. But you must agree that some people like to complicate things, because it makes them look smart. The less we understand something, the more we dig the hole of overcomplicated logic in an effort to explain what we are too embarrassed to admit we cannot.

People also complicate matters, as I do myself, because it is not enough to know the car works when I turn the key. I feel a need to look at the engine and figure out how and why it works. I am glad I do not feel that way about color TV and especially HD, because I would go crazy trying to get to the bottom of that technology. I only know that it does work when I click the remote. Some of us, in other words, complicate things because by nature we are full of questions and have been since childhood. It is the adult version of the infamous why.

We start to ask all kinds of questions, some of which seem reasonable to ask. We cannot simply accept the main unifying Christian idea that Jesus died for me. That seems too simplistic. No, we need to know details. As regards this thing called salvation, when does it take place? Is it gradual? Is reconciliation with God a developing thing, as we learn to appreciate what happened at Calvary? Is anything else important? What about Baptism? How and when? What about going to church? Giving money? Are these important? Things get involved when we try to figure out how the thing Jesus did on the day He died, whatever it was, works for us. Each one of these minutiae or added tidbits of Christian thought become so important to us.

No wonder you might have walked away shaking your head.

Let me catch up to you, not to convince you of anything, but to apologize for explaining things I knew I couldn't explain. My generation maintained that we believed something, because it changed our lives. The basic truth about Christ dying for us did change us. But lots of these added tweaks to our sermons were only head-stuff, designed to make us look more knowledgeable than someone else.

Some topics needed to be tweaked, in our erroneous way of thinking, to support our interests. When, for example, grammar supported two possible meanings to a scripture verse, we picked the one that was on our side. We even chose college textbooks and Bible translations we felt supported us. We would deny other possible interpretations had merit. I have known serious scholarship to support this approach, as if it were a great debate rather than a hunger to get at the truth.

One teacher I had, for whom I will forever have the greatest respect and admiration and who will always be my mentor, Professor Grazier, reviewed a certain grammatical construction for me. He told me that everywhere it appeared in the New Testament, he concluded that his denomination's view was the only one possible. Later, I read the New Testament through from cover to cover, in the original language, and I found about a half dozen possible exceptions.

I'm sorry for boring you with technical babble, which you probably don't care about, but you must have had a gut feeling that something wasn't being said right over the years. In Sunday School or in church, you knew all along, but were too young to realize, that you had stumbled upon it, that some religious differences were made-up. They were introduced to give you a sense of privilege or pride in being in the church you were in. Some have even gone so far as to suggest a divine wrath or punishment for even visiting a different Christian church.

I was a teenager when my younger sister invited her friend to our church, only to have the friend tearfully tell us she couldn't. She was told it was a sin.

Another case I remember was a woman who came to our church— not the denomination of her childhood—on the invitation of her husband. She was told by members of her first family that the ceiling would collapse on her in God's displeasure. She told me she feared the roof would cave in when she first stepped into the building. Obviously, it didn't.

Consequent to all of this, whole Bible topics were off-limits, because they did not support denominational ideas. Whole sections of Scripture we skipped over, because we had no way to explain these in the light of what we believed. Even Martin Luther, whom I referenced already, struggled with the Epistle of James. He wanted to deny its inspiration or remove it from the canon altogether, because it seemed to emphasize a view he did not support. It was too Catholic.

Some portions of the Bible are too Baptist or too Pentecostal or too pick-your-theological-poison to risk bringing into the wrong pulpit at the wrong time.

My problem was that different faiths taught me different, still important aspects of truth. As a Baptist minister in Dedham, I learned a slant on some Scriptures that made the truth they contained clearer and more exciting, and yet I never wanted to disown my Pentecostal heritage.

I found much to be desired in both faiths. At Duquesne University I also taught a Catholic group during the charismatic conference of 1979. I found those Christians the greatest delight to teach. My regard for Catholics who share with me a passion for truth grew exponentially.

I suppose, for God to fix this intellectual mess, He would first have to minimize the scholar's input. He first has to shut us up. More music and less theological positioning, perhaps, would be in order, because we have choruses in common. We used to use hymnbooks peculiar to our denomination, from our publishing company. Maybe today's guitars and PowerPoint presentations are a first step on God's part to bring us all back to the simple message He had in the first place. I don't say this in ridicule but in hope. For example, at "In the Deep," a monthly worship event at a local Pentecostal church, most of the participants come from other, non-Pentecostal churches. This approach may be the only way God can bring about Christian unity.

Yes, some teachers of God's Word were open about their studies, but open scholarship was rare when our generation was at the religious helm. True scholarship will admit its limited understanding or that some-one of another view has Biblical grounds for his view. Some knew that there was more to learn than what they had discovered. They were in-nately aware of some who had insight into areas of truth they had not been able to focus on.

Religious teachers, if they are honest, realize that in some ways they are specialists. There is no way they could understand every thought and every idea behind every verse of Scripture. Only God has that kind of in-sight and knowledge. It is now my opinion that true scholarship should pick some area of Biblical study, and if it does a good job, it will relate that study to the message of the death and resurrection of Jesus Christ.

This keeps our focus on this one message and brings about unity. It also makes my apology easier to express. I simply want to say I am sorry that we allowed many of our children to grow up in our churches, leav-ing them without the demonstrated message of God's love. We may have given you no legacy that we could be proud of.

It didn't help me to love being with (in alphabetical order) Baptists, Catholics, Pentecostals, and Presbyterians alike. It didn't help me to care about the church down the street. I preached a sermon on one occasion that sent a family packing back to the church they left. And I was happy about that, because they needed to reconcile and go on with their lives there, not here with us. It didn't help me to promote a general church growth among all Christians, if it meant my excitement over the blessing

133

that was somewhere else.

It didn't help me to attempt honesty in the pulpit when I wasn't sure what the verse said, or I was sure and it wasn't what our denomination wanted to hear. But I had a much bigger problem. The pain of rejection got to me. I wanted everyone to like me. I had a hard time saying, "No."

No is a Good Word

Learn to say No.
It will be of more use to you than to be able to read Latin.
--Charles Haddon Spurgeon

C.S. Lewis wrote in March 1948, "From the longing to be thought well of... from the fear of being rejected, deliver me, Jesus."

No is a good word, but for political reasons, for their own future hopes in a given church, pastors find themselves saying "Yes" instead. We agree with people who are in the wrong, but who are in power too.

Let me explain. A church is a group of people, and therefore, by definition, it is a political entity, with a government. In the churches I pastored, government meant elected officials, including the pastor. Some other pastors are appointed by colleagues. A few pastors can claim a divine calling, and have the personality, respect, and empowerment to make it stick. But many pastors are elected by congregations. In some churches, the pastor's license is legal simply because the congregation voted him in.

The degree of political maneuvering or the ability of a pastor to lead may be directly related to the form of the church's government. If things start falling apart for a minister, there may be more empathy and protection among colleagues than among parishioners. On the other hand, it may not go well if the vote of confidence is with the very congregation that is displeased with its leadership.

I have to admit my confusion when one congregation I pastored was organizing for such a vote during a presidential election year. I honestly wondered if people were caught up in the passion of national issues and directing their fury toward me and my family. I wonder, does a small boy's playing on a church lawn deserve the same serious address as the national debt? I believe it happened that way.

When church leaders prepare for the vote, there should be a rule that allows the children to share in the decision-making process because they will share in the decision. Their little lives are as open as their parents' to scrutiny. They are open as well for criticism and all the hurt that can flow out of a meeting gone wrong.

Yes, politics is a part of the church because it involves people, and the majority of any group bears a great weight of decision even if it is not immediately evident. William Schaeffer referred to this as a dictatorship

135

of 51 percent.

Dare I open the curtains of a cute little house owned by a member of a small but growing church and observe a meeting in progress? Seated around a prominent member of the church, perhaps a deacon, is a group of mostly ladies. In this church, the women outnumbered the men 2 to 1. The ladies are expressing their disapproval of the current pastor and agreeing that something has to be done about it. This is no meaningless exercise. It will snowball, until the pastor will decide to leave. True story.

One way or another, through boards or through the grapevine, influential people have a lot to say. That message may be based on experience or education. It might come from a deep hurt or be influenced by the passions of others. No matter: it is there. One teacher gave it a fancy name which I only mention here, "the nomothetic dimension." Do what you want with that.

"Damned if you do, and damned if you don't," the saying goes. There is some truth to that, if a pastor has to support an idea his gut says is wrong, which means he will have been intimidated, or come against it, which could be political and professional suicide. Pastors do dig holes for themselves. Sometimes they don't even know that they are doing it.

A perfectly good sermon enrages a board member or Sunday School teacher. They accuse the pastor of publicly directing his accusations against them, when in all honesty he wasn't even thinking of them. It gets difficult to stay open to the Bible message in preparing and presenting homilies and sermons when the pastor has to tiptoe around Bible verses because they sound accusing. Who knew? A message that should have gone well and would have in another church not only bombs but genuinely offends. It has happened to me.

If the people are not happy, and pastors spend centuries defining happiness in doctrinal terms to certain parishioners, the parishioners leave, and so does their money, and that's church politics for you.

Pastors need pulpit amnesty. At least in the absence of evidence to the contrary, shouldn't they have the benefit of the doubt? Maybe they were bringing God's message for the moment, and maybe it was for someone other than the offended party. The same respect should be granted pastors as is given to visiting preachers, who can say practically anything and get away with it. The rule of thumb should be: speak in love. I think I read that somewhere in Paul's writings.

Sometimes, pastors do have ulterior motives for saying what they say in the pulpit, but not usually, and that's another talk. Here, we are looking at a congregation's response to a message delivered in humble honesty as inspired scripture.

One minister told me that I was fortunate because there were some things he could not say in his pulpit but for some reason he was sure I could. Go figure.

Pastors also don't have the privilege of silence. After all, their mouth is what makes their ministry, or breaks it. Pastors also need to take sides on issues, just like candidates for political office. They must say what and why is their position, even on matters they have not had time to prayerfully study through. If the congregation is split down the middle, it may be the beginning of the end. When, for example, abortion first became a national political issue, it had to be addressed by the church and therefore by its pastors, and therefore, by me.

Within the church itself, the same could be said about doctrinal positions that have divided congregations for generations. Many of these issues were theological. Half the time, my convictions and study led me in the wrong direction, politically speaking.

Many of the examples here are from my own experience. The purpose behind relating these accounts is not venting bad feelings, because I have none. My ability to remain angry is like a computer's memory with the power off. Memories can be good to us even if they were painful, because we are allowed to learn good lessons from them. We are allowed to mature through the experiences, so our memories become on reflection a weird sort of blessing.

We have to be careful not to imply that church people are bad people and that pastors are victims of a hurtful political system. There is an intrinsic difference between discussion, which is good, and in-fighting, which is not. There's a difference between a democratic vote (the system) and uniting around leadership (the imperative), between honoring the pastor (the opportunity) and respecting the office (the requirement). We used to go beyond the intended reason for church government and church constitutions. We often used church government for personal gain, not for the benefit of others, and that's how church leadership can and did abuse the system. People think, now that I am in power, I will do things my way. This though lacks the sensitivity to genuinely care about those who follow. Leaders must learn first to be servants, or the system works against itself.

Church politics also involves leaks about matters not intended for the public ear. We call it gossip, one of the things wrong with our generation of churchgoers. Advice given in the pastor's office in secret becomes the topic of sewing circles. The grapevine knows a lot and has an opinion. Many other private matters become public topics, and it is not un-common for a pastor to favor the public view without a second thought. He anticipates the inevitable, that something will leak out, so he decides to go with the flow and protect himself from ridicule. It doesn't matter what happens to the counseled. Sometimes this works out well for every-one, because the counseled shouldn't have been in the pastor's chambers to start with. Some people are better served by other professionals, by people more knowledgeable of their particular situation, or by someone onto whom they are less likely to transfer affection. Sometimes, however, we drop-kick out of our world someone we should be helping. The need is genuine and we are in a unique position to meet it but we fear for our reputation.

Sometimes, I had a congregation's opinion telling me that I had blown it. Other times, wisdom ruled, and we had amazing success. I was actually proud of some counseling I gave, because the results were heal-ing. It made me think that I knew what I was doing, Other sessions did-n't fare so well, when either people did not heed the advise, or I gave foolish counsel—at least according to the grapevine.

Pastors make another mistake. They might contradict the principles they preach and live by in order to please people, in hopes that the storm will blow over. It is a delicate balancing act that is designed to keep dea-cons happy, while still leading. Influential church members ask the pas-tor to do something that violates his principles or that he has a gut feeling he shouldn't do, and then he does it, to stay on the good side of some un-wise adviser. This is called intimidation, and I have been guilty of being intimidated, probably more so than some.

Examples of this are easy to come by for all pastors. I remember one elderly gentleman who showed an interest in returning to our fellowship. One of the deacons told me to inform him of a rule he was breaking. My gut said, "Don't do it," but I did it anyhow. The man packed up and walked out for good. I had his funeral soon after. This is a very sad mem-ory.

We are often pressured to say things, whether in sermon or individ-ual counsel. It comes with the job. We have to learn at all costs to follow our gut. We have to learn not to allow ourselves to be intimidated into a decision we do not want to make. Giving in to intimidation labels us as having no principles. Intimidation kills, professionally.

I had to learn to say, "No."

Pulpit Etiquette

Perfect behavior is born of complete indifference.
~Cesare Pavese, This Business of Living: Diaries

"Oh! That I could wear out of my mind every mean and base affection, conquer my natural pride and conceit," wrote our second President, John Adams. On July 21, 1756, he wrote, "I am resolved to rise with the sun and to study Scriptures... I will rouse up my mind... I will strive with all my soul to be something..."

But the next morning, according to his biographer, David McCullough, who collected this note from Adam's diary, Adams slept until seven and wrote, "A very rainy day. Dreamed away the time."

How spontaneously human we are!

During the enthusiasm of one sermon, I leaned into the microphone, and in a revealing tone I declared, "After all, I'm not God." Then I went on with whatever the topic was. That one comment impressed one member in a singular way. She thought it to be one of the clearest and nicest and perhaps most inspired things a preacher ever said to a congregation. She thanked me with a spontaneity that made it clear to me that she was not being sarcastic or just nice. She meant it. So did I. I noticed over the years that parishioners like seeing my human side in my sermons. Church leadership expressed concern, however, since I was supposed to be "God's voice."

It is difficult to admit the obvious, that pastors are mere humans, with our own moral and ethical weaknesses to deal with. So if people ever knew that I yelled at you boys or got furious at Mom or took off all night sulking about how neglected I was, they would no doubt feel that I their pastor knew how they lived and what they faced.

Preachers need to be careful here. I'll offer you a smidgen of psychological insight into the thoughts of a minister when they are preaching about personal experiences. Some sermons are preached from a hurting conscience, not from a position of strength and commitment. Watch out for sermons on sex or loving your spouse. These can be very uncomfortable, even scary, pulpit moments for the people, who must be wondering what the preacher is getting at. The pulpit mike can provide a soapbox from which to vent feelings. It can even carry a desperate but unconscious call for prayer from a preacher in emotional trouble.

I avoided most of those pitfalls, I think. I purposely avoided talking about sex. I was vulnerable, though, to an Old Testament woe now and again, when my depression would kick in. People on the attack can pull the word woe right out of almost any preacher's mouth.

Pastors also live with fears, doubts, and even hate at times, which they are not at liberty to share openly. When a certain elder was once injured in an auto accident, I had actually hoped he would die. I repented of this thought, but not publicly. Still, any of these feelings could surface in a message. So when the pastor starts overemphasizing the need to trust and not fear, perhaps that is God's message to the preacher, and you are privileged to eavesdrop on the conversation.

Some sermons a pastor avoids because he doesn't know from experience what to say. I couldn't preach on fasting, not ever. Wonder why? I loved food too much. I gained thirty pounds overnight, it seemed, and maintained it with no effort at all. Similarly, you'll seldom hear a message on speaking in tongues from someone who doesn't.

So what's the secret to a good sermon? A good life. To the degree the person in the pulpit messes up or lives below the Biblical standard of good ethics and morals, they run the risk of bringing their pain and guilt with them before their congregation and saying things that are not divinely inspired.

"Did I ever do this?" you ask. Probably, but my bigger problem was my awareness of this dynamic in-pulpit ministry and the stress of trying to avoid airing my dirty laundry in public. When preachers hold back this way, their message can become oversimplified and vague. After all, the content of a good sermon is morals and ethics. Their words tends to lack substance, and when the people are used to getting substance and don't get it, they have to know that something is amiss.

I did have my fights with Mom, and my concerns about life, and my temptations. I did try to present a realistic picture of life, and yes, I often used myself as an example. But I came right out and told people if something bothered me. I made it an important point in my sermon. I didn't want to hint at something I was doing wrong without consciously telling anyone that I was doing it. I didn't use charades or intentionally bring my guilt into the pulpit so it could flavor my words. I tried to avoid this scene, so truth be told, I would do my real sinning on Monday. This gave me all week to repent and get my act together before the weekend. Saturday night, or worse yet Sunday morning, was the worst time to come apart. I would wait until Monday.

So what did I do on Monday that was so bad?

Monday was when I would get my weekly depression. I think it was

of the mild endogenous type, probably because I was coming down emotionally from the weekend high. But I did enjoy the self-attention and the
time off. I could also bring one on at times with an accompanying
headache, if I wanted an excuse to cancel something.

Under the influence of such a need for attention, I was capable of almost any selfish act, and your poor mother had to endure my advances
and pleadings. Your old man was quite human when it came right down
to it. He didn't always do or think the biblical thing.

While in the pulpit, however, we were supposed to be the voice of
God, even if we were wrong or weren't sure whether we were right or
wrong. We were not supposed to admit that any part of our sermon
could have been simply how we felt or what we thought at the time. It all
had to be from God. Don't admit otherwise! Sometimes it was clear to us
that the point we were making was our own opinion, but we dasn't say
so. I betrayed my humanness one Sunday by admitting that my comments were my view of Scripture, and I received a delightful reprimand
afterward from one parishioner.

We denied personal opinion or ignorance or any notion that suggested anything we said while in the pulpit might have been us. We could
play it safe by taking into our pulpits standard theological concepts that
were favored by the denomination we were in and present them as pure
gospel. We thereby would deal with no contradiction and no chance of
saying something wrong or offensive.

Well, the older I became, the less sure I became that this approach
was the right approach. With the years, I longed for more discussion and
less dogma, more of a desire to learn than to teach, more intellectual honesty and less enlisting scripture in support of an idea. And I wanted the
Bible to speak to our humanness.

I have given up now on theological distinctives, interpretations of
Scripture that are intended to support one church and prove another
wrong. I hope to eventually reach an age, if I live long enough, where
even those parts of the Bible that offend our ethical or moral sensitivity,
like the Song of Solomon, will no longer be excluded from the overall
message. Some Scripture is raw, but it has to be to make its point. Just say
it, and let the old ladies deal with it as best they can.

I learned in all of this a serious lesson about pulpit etiquette, and I
am not referring to the way a preacher stands there or moves his hands.
When I have the pulpit, I want the boldness of my convictions, and not
care what anyone thinks of me. If I know that I have put forth my best effort to understand what the Bible is saying, and I can present that mes-

sage with a clear conscience, then I am fulfilled. And if someone has another opinion, they have a right to that opinion. Let them find their own pulpit.

At least then, if people are upset with me, they are upset with the real me. If I can go into the pulpit with conviction, that has to be the best I can do, for after all, I'm not God.

I Made Some Regrettable Decisions

A man is not old until his regrets take the place of his dreams
--a proverb

Do I have any regrets? I have two different kinds of the stuff since by personality I tend to be melancholic. There are things I wish had gone differently, as for example, having a real opportunity to go into some Seminary and get a couple advanced degrees. This door closed abruptly in 1969, when I graduated from NBI. The year before, an NBI graduate raised a theological storm at the seminary I wanted to attend, and the powers that be thought it best to wait at least one year before accepting anyone else from our little Institute.

The worse type of regret is the thing someone does wrong or says in bad taste, and he wishes he could retrieve the moment and rerun it. I've had a few of these. I walked away from a few people I hurt and didn't even look back to see if they were crying. (Include a girlfriend or two in this list.)

In August 1965, I gave my uncle, having already spent a lifetime being each other's best friend, about three weeks notice of my leaving for Bible school. He asked me to reconsider, but of course I couldn't. A week later he was found asleep on his couch, and he couldn't be awakened. If loneliness can kill, I have proof.

I regret running away to Greenlane the weekend prior to my dad's death. I still feel there was a connection between my leaving for Greenlane and his death. That is one of my biggest regrets.

I guess like everyone else, I do live with regret, and now I hope for a heaven in order to be able to make things right in the next life.

Did I regret Butler? It's not the point of this narrative to answer that, only to raise the question because we all live with similar inquiries into our past, more particularly into those decisions we made that appeared to lead us and our family directly into hurt and want.

But did I regret Butler? If there is going to be healing and a healthy looking forward to better times, we need to answer a big fat "NO!" to such questions. We might be in those better times already but not recognize it, because we are blinded by bad memories and a lingering bitter feeling left by them. It is as if someone needs to be punished for what happened, because it was wrong, maybe even criminal, and since there is no one else we can beat up on, we beat up on ourselves. We need to learn to live in the present.

Do I have any regrets about you boys? None! You boys are my life. At one point in our journey all three of you unconsciously joined in to keep my feet on the ground when I was slipping into (probably) a clinical depression. The worst never did happen, in large part thanks to you.

Any regrets about mom? No. I love mom, and I cannot imagine being married to another woman. My sole regret is that we did not have opportunity to stretch out our engagement. Life got too serious too quickly for two young adults unprepared for it all.

How permanent or forever were my dumb decisions? Their influence on my future can be minimized if I can learn from them.

Do I look back and say, "I never made a good decision"? I think not. I made a lot of good ones. Life might have taken a different turn if I had stayed here or there instead of moving again. I didn't have to leave the little town of Burgettstown. Who knew that a small community, probably not on most maps, would one day be visited by the President of the United States, and I missed it. I didn't have to leave Sharon, PA when we lived there. It was another decision to move to Massachusetts.

I only know, here I am with my family, and your families, and my grandchildren about me. If these people who are important to me love me and, yes, where necessary, forgive me, I am right where I need to be and want to be.

I think in terms of my wants, I would like an opportunity to be in the pulpit again, even though I know that presents a challenge all its own. This would not be an easy thing, since the church is changing around me.

I did do some things that were regrettable.

We borrowed money once from an alleged member of the New York underworld. Glad we paid it back on schedule.

I once visited a lady in the church, alone. I had thought she was in her 60's when she had visited the church with her grandchildren. They were her children. She was in her early thirties, and her gray hair was actually platinum blond. I heard her out, prayed with her and got the heck out of there but too late. The town had already heard.

I argued with a credentials committee one time. I might have been right. I proceeded to establish my position, using Greek syntax, to a group of men who probably did not have a clue what I was saying. The chairman or General Presbyter had had six weeks formal education in Bible at a summer camp. They called me theologically vague and my ordination was held up for years.

I was not a Lucy Ricardo, but I made gaffes and then tried to solve the problems they got me into. Sometimes my stupidity was simply raw honesty about something said in a sermon, something guaranteed to offend. But is it stupid to be honest? Or is there an honest but smart answer that can get a guy out of the trouble he is getting himself into?

Called to a joint meeting of presbyters, deacons, and a few trustees, I was asked regarding my position on a particular theological topic. I knew what they wanted to hear, but in my head, as a matter of principle, I wanted to be honest, as if I'd never told a lie. I clarified what I understood the Bible to be saying. I later phoned Professor Grazier and told him all about it. His comment: "Why didn't you tell them what they wanted hear?"

Of course, no man makes a decision in a vacuum. Not just thought goes into making it but also, I think, his past experience and his personality, and even his associates may share a part. My past experiences, as I sadly mentioned already, left me with an inferior view of myself, which opened the door to being intimidated. My associates often came up with ideas that I bought into that seemed reasonable and sensible at the time but turned out to be regrettably stupid.

Many of my ideas were probably not my ideas after all. I might have been taking someone else's advice because it sounded good. The line sometimes became blurred between what was in my head, or in another's with whom I took counsel. For example, my uncle blamed your grandma for my interest in Bible school. It was public knowledge that she wished she had become a missionary, and now she wanted her son to take her place. I only know that with independent thought, I do not regret Bible school.

Hey! I met Mom there!

Sorry is a natural word for me, so I probably see bad in a few good decisions.

Sometimes, I am sorry for something I didn't do or say. Sometimes when others accuse me, there is a part of me that can agree with them.. Remember Mr. Hurd on the Bob Newhart show? In one episode he becomes angered at Mr Carlin, a member of his support group. Bob, the psychologist, commends him for his anger, something he never shows. After the session, out in the waiting area, Mr. Carlin continues his abusive verbal assault on Mr Hurd. Now in outright rage, Mr. Hurd grabs the knitting needles from Mrs. Bakerman's sewing bag, and sticks himself with them.

This whole scene is psychologically sad. I know it is good only to take what you know you have coming and refuse the rest. And I know abuse is never good. But over the years, possibly in an effort to placate a combatant or mitigate someone's anger, I would accept blame so that I could start the apologies and bring a quick reconciliation.

The absolute rule is to accept responsibility only for what you have done, whether good or bad. Let people work their anger out. Let them rant on, even if it is exhausting work to sit there and argue your innocence. Get to the bottom of the truth always, and if others cannot accept that, leave them to their Maker.

I did and said enough stupid things without others piling on additional blame. I had plenty of opportunity to apologize for real, and I think the biggest of these apologies is right here in this letter, to you boys. I sincerely wish there could be a way to take 40 years of learned wisdom back into the past with me and redo a few things, to make life a lot easier for you.

There is a ton of good in people, and that includes Christians. There is much to commend the Bible they want to promote, even if they—we—do a poor job advertising its value. And I still believe God can show Himself to us in a way capable of convincing us that He is real and that He really cares. Give Him the chance, always, no matter what happened in the past.

The Church is Changing

Wisdom doesn't automatically come with old age.
Nothing does - except wrinkles.
--Abigail Van Buren

What did God have in mind when He began His church? Just maybe a generation of Christians has arrived that will reconsider this question and be prepared to make bold steps in redefining the church's role in society. In short, today's young church could be ready to correct a number of mistakes that has characterized Christianity over the centuries.

If there is any truth to this, we must be careful not to understand this generation in terms of the last. Take a look at the more evident differences. We attended always in Sunday, go-to-meeting clothes. It was not as today, where everyone comes in jeans during the colder seasons and in shorts when it's hot out. We promoted the idea, nowhere found in the Bible, that cleanliness is next to Godliness. Wearing a tie was a spiritually revealing thing to do. We had suits only for Sunday service. They went along with the ties. How refreshing to remember Shorty. Most Sundays, he came to service in a tee shirt. There is really nothing wrong with that. Today, people attend in very casual wear (sometimes even the preacher), and they may even be carrying a cup of java or something else to sip during the sermon.

Today's church is different. We tended to turn people away, and not just because their beliefs differed from ours. We informed one young woman, who wanted to come to church, that she couldn't attend unless she wore a dress. But the only dress she owned was very short, and she was too self-conscious wearing it. So she stayed home. Today, women come to church in denim.

We cringed when, one Sunday, in walked a young woman wearing a hooker outfit. She was invited, and that was the only dress she owned. We made an issue out of long hair for men, never mind earrings and tattoos. We got bent out of shape over a cigarette butt discovered on the front church steps, or something spilled on the carpet in the basement. We were offended by poor folk whose dress and sometimes fragrance was not up to code. Remember, "cleanliness is next to Godliness." We were simply overwhelmed with disinterest when someone came in smelling of alcohol. Some inner city ministries were trained to deal with that sort of thing. We moved to the suburbs and small towns to get away

147

from it.

I can't see these things happening in today's church, where people hold coffee cups in seats—not pews, where they wear shorts, where preachers put on simple but life-relevant PowerPoint presentations and song leaders sing simple songs—and sometimes not so simple—played with guitars and drums (loud drums). We sing to electric guitars, and the organ is gone. The grand piano in some churches has also been replaced with electronic synthesizers. And there is frequently a small choir of voices, each with their own microphone, instead of a single song leader.

The Bible belt might be the last bastion for hymnbooks, and yesteryear's songs about the blood of Christ, and other once popular topics that have been replaced by choruses about worship and faith. It probably was a natural progression since today's singer probably doesn't want to strain their vocal chords in four sharps and do it for four or five stanzas. In fact, I don't think today's songs come in four stanzas. Do they?

The biggest change that has taken place is acceptance. You are not given to feel unwelcome anymore because of your looks or fragrance. It seems they want you there. The larger churches have developed a number of different groups, one of which will probably accommodate you as a visitor. They have categorized you by age and sex and whatever else warrants another group. They maintain support groups for addictions and even a ministry for the homeless in some cases. The smaller churches simply provide a friendlier environment because they want you there.

The most dynamic change I see is the lack of fighting over doctrine. Some of the older debates have simply faded away. I must admit that I do not know anymore what label a Christian wears, if he wears one at all. The Pentecostals have toned it down, and the Baptists are clapping their hands these days, so the war might be coming to an end.

Thank God!

And what about science and evolution? The last sermon I heard on the subject, the preacher endorsed theistic evolution. He maintained that evolution is real and that God is behind it. I wonder how popular that idea is. I think it is safe to at least suggest that the war between science and the church is also coming to an end. And I am grateful for that, too. There never really was any conflict between the church's message and scientific inquiry and research.

Don't tell the IRS, but generally I have observed in recent years that trustee boards serve a lesser role than they once did. They still pay the bills, but they don't own the checkbooks. Pastors are defining their interests in ministry and congregations are rallying behind the vision they represent, so that trustees have no choice but to sign the checks and go home.

But the biggest change seen with today's generation of Christians is their spontaneous interest in the simple Bible message and their total lack of interest in arguing theological minutiae. This is a marked difference from yesterday's believer. If we profile this modern-day Christian, we start to notice a trend toward unity, since the distinctives embodied in those minutiae, which defined the denominations these minutiae represented, are no longer important. Pastors are even legally changing the corporate name or title of the churches they pastor, in order to remove any denominational connection. More churches are simply labeled "community" churches to underscore this trend.

And what about scholarship? What about Greek and Hebrew? What about the King James Bible or the Rheims-Douay translation? It is my opinion that since the Biblical Greek and Classical Hebrew were the unwilling servants of religious difference, it has also been relegated to a lesser role. Perhaps such scholarship is a dying interest. Its survival now, I believe, depends on the ability of today's scholar to employ it in an open and honest interest in understanding the message of Scripture which was written for one church, united.

Bible translations? Today's pastor uses a number of them, depending on his audience, in an effort to simply explain the message inherent in Scripture.

So I see a movement toward the simplicity and emphasis of the Biblical message, which was always God's intention. I see people gathering in small groups, wearing comfortable clothes, and if they choose, bringing with them something to eat or drink. I see more dialog and happier times, because I see fewer fights and fewer board meetings of any consequence. Even congregational meetings are mostly an excuse to gather for fellowship. I even see the money serving a wiser end, because the focus is less and less denominational and more and more community-oriented.

Do I like these changes? Not all of them. I miss the organ music and some of the old hymns. I miss that certain old-fashioned atmosphere that came along with a nineteenth-century building and pews and stained glass. I personally miss some of the people with whom I once worshiped, some of them still living, and some of those, not that far from me. I am not especially impressed with some of the newness, some of the new choruses which I cannot harmonize to. And everyone wants to greet me with coffee and donuts. What's that all about? I especially miss an in-depth

Bible study. I like the Greek and Hebrew stuff. PowerPoint is a very new thing, and it doesn't really do anything for me. But I admit this is my age talking. This is a cultural discomfort that has no relevance when one considers what church is really all about.

I know I am now the old grouch, the crotchety, gray-haired codger who calls "wrong" anything he doesn't like.

Please, Lord, not me! I prefer to recognize that today's generation has a right to their style of worship as much as I had mine. The main point worth noting here is that some of the changes just might be a providential design at work to unite people who could not hold hands before. When things are said and done, we might witness the greatest and most irrefutable proof that God is real, one Church.

PART FIVE
Epilogue

It may not have been perfectly clear, especially during times of unexplainable hurt, but in the most absolute sense of the phrase, always, your mother and I have loved you.

We had made decisions at times that belied this fact. And yes, in the church some of those decisions, now looking back with shameful regret, were politically motivated. I tried to please people. It didn't always work, as well you know. But never ever were these—even the bad—moves made without a look in your direction. We couldn't make them as if you were not there.

If Jesus had His inner circle, I had mine: my family. One of my favorite verses is Genesis 6:18, in which God says to Noah, "I solemnly swear to keep you safe in the boat, with your wife and your sons and their wives." This verse has been the sum of my life's interest. Sure, I would like an ark big enough to rescue countless others, but I need to know my sons, my wife, and my son's wives and their families are in it, too.

We knew sometimes you hurt, and that increased our pain. Within the limit of our resources, you have to know, however, we did what we could to give you the world.

Now it may have come to this, the most cherished thing I have, which I may have failed to impart to you, my faith, faith in an eternal God who loves us. Regretfully, I may have failed to show you that the Christian life and church life are not at all the same, that God and church people do not always see eye to eye, that there is sometimes a difference between trusting in Him and endorsing what the church believes. You grew up in the church, when your mother and I wanted you to grow up in Him.

I have not been too much into the Bible stories of things like the Garden of Eden or Noah's ark. It seems right that science wants to investigate the evidence in these accounts. So your understanding of these stories is not the traditional position. I don't care. I have nothing here to defend. I believe that ultimately mankind will have his answer.

What about heaven and hell? I know next to nothing about them. I have to believe that in some sense they are real places. My problem is that I am convinced Jesus spoke of them in some sense or in some way that makes them real. Church people like to imagine what these places are like. I think heaven is heaven because the God of love is active there. I hope I get to walk among flowers and sit under large trees with no mosquitoes. Hell, on the under hand, is a nightmare to me. God's love is not active there. But these are general impressions, not clear truth.

I have three main beliefs: One, that God exists. Two, that He loves us. Three, that the Bible somehow, even if the wording isn't 100% accurate in translation, or even if a word or two is missing from our copy, is God's book. He, I believe—and I can not explain it adequately—authored it, or at least endorses it as His genuine position on life. It represents what in life should be important to us, for it is important to Him. I always and only wanted to see Him in its pages and share that insight with you. I have hoped to observe the God of the Book. I thought it valuable to see what excited or enraged Him. So, I have cared much more to investigate those parts of the Bible that say something about His life and ours.

Much of this truth is already a part of you, because the Bible has a profound insight into life, and you already show this insight. It is wisdom to follow many of its principles. Love your wife, for one, is an idea that I believe you have all exemplified. This speaks volumes, not only about your integrity, of which I have been very proud, but also your admittance that Scripture does have something important to offer.

If I have any legacy, I hope it is this: that, aside from God and family, my most cherished possession since a child has been the Bible. Ever since about 6 years of age, when I copied its lettering from somewhere in the middle of an open Bible, I have been warmly drawn to the mystery of its meaning. I have wept over its revelation of salvation. I have thrilled over its inspiration. I have longed to know its less popular verses. I have hungered to learn it in the language it was originally written. And if I could share a portion of that excitement with you, my life would not have been lived for nothing. I never cared about money or a lot of expensive, fun things. You can count on one hand the times we went to an amusement park. I never cared about church things, either. I guess that was my administrative downfall. I only wanted to get into the Bible and pursue my one and only interest in ministry.

They called me a teacher. If so, that skill or calling alone was not enough to qualify me to be a pastor in today's world. I was okay with that. Through this insight, I was able to learn something about myself that should have been evident all along. I found out that learning Scripture was my vision. I had most literally and explicitly no other interest in the church. Learning the Book and living its message was church to me.

154

It may have been a lot of other things to others, but I wouldn't know that.

You may not know that for me the Christian experience is very private. I do not mean by that that I wouldn't want someone else to know about it. I mean that the God I want to know is not some philosophical idea extracted from some college text. He is to me the God found in the Old Testament. In those pages, God seems very personable. He calls David a friend and speaks face to face with Moses. He and Moses actually argue. And after dinner with Abraham, He takes a walk under the night sky to talk about Abraham's future. They converse about Lot, Abraham's nephew, in terms that suggest God isn't sure what He wants to do. This provides Abraham with an opportunity to discuss it. We call it prayer, and this is one of the most dynamic prayers I have ever read about. Elsewhere, God yells, cries, gets angry, jumps for joy, becomes indecisive, and repents, among other feelings and actions that reveal a God who wants to get to our level. Enoch simply walked with Him.

This God is for real.

This God I want to know, if knowing Him is possible. But this is a very private relationship. When I pray to Him, I talk to Him. And I am not on my knees. I am on the train or walking down the street. My conversations with Him are very private. This makes my public prayer life mostly ceremonial and staged, because in private I say things to God that I would never want to become public. Some people probably think I am just talking to myself, that the whole experience is just as healing or cathartic or stress reducing as talking at the grave site of a loved one. I quite obviously disagree.

The saying goes: Don't knock it until you've tried it. And that's what I say. Give God a chance to reveal Himself. Talk to Him and see if He can find a way in His wisdom to talk back.

Each one of us is different. What works to convince me of the reality of this relationship with God won't work necessarily with you. The way God lets me know that He is real or that He is there probably wouldn't prove a thing to you, so my witness becomes weak in that sense. Some people get excited to hear about a burning bush—familiar story?—or a life-changing event or such like. They think nothing could better prove the love of God. And yet, to others of a more scientific mindset, these events may range from myth to co-incidence.

This is okay. God has to accept the challenge of talking back. He has to find a way to reveal who He is, if He can, if He will. All I am saying here is to give Him a chance. Cut Him enough slack that you are willing to entertain some doubt as to the idea that God doesn't exist, and that if

He exists, maybe He lives in a different reality than we do, and just maybe He wants to cross the chasm that separates our realities and contact us.

Sounds more science-fiction than spiritual, doesn't it? Here, however, is where a lot of our reality first lived before science discovered it. Man has always had an inquisitive mind, and this curiosity has already invented technology that 100 years ago would have been an unbelievable future. Yet, it is here. Science has pieced together elements from the past that have painted a very detailed picture of life before man. We now know something about the beginnings of the universe as well. Universities hold courses in parapsychology. (I am not exactly sure what that is.) And we are concerned about our children's future with some reasonably good scientific concerns.

How can we be so intelligent and not consider God? How is everything else possible but Him?

No, it is the scientific mind, not the religious one that should be inquiring after Him. This is all I ask of you.

What has worked for me? When I was a teenager, I began to doubt God's existence. The church didn't help me much to find reassurance. I found it in grammar, of all things. I won't attempt to bore you with details, but I became convinced in the uniqueness of the Bible to the world of literature. I saw miracles taking place in the historical development of the languages in which the Bible was eventually written. All of this added support to my conversations with God as we walked.

My prayer is that you, too, will walk with God. You will discover the relationship which I am convinced alone offers us an eternal future together. Together with Him and you is what I look forward to.

See you there.

Love,

Dad.

PART SIX

Appendices

Some things might be worth saying, but they were not germane to my story. These might be the between-the-lines comments, things you wondered about or on which you wanted further clarity. I list four of them here.

Tithing was a dreaded topic through the years for me, because I felt the church abused the concept. Sorry for the thought, but it gave me no small amount of stress. I struggled to find any common ground sufficient for both them and me to live in harmony.

The defense of the Gospel is to me an oxymoron. The gospel message is the sword and doesn't require defending, only wielding. So when extra doctrines arose to defend one Christian group from another, I found myself in the line of fire. I couldn't get out of the way.

What is Christianity? I had a history teacher who struggled with this question and finally came up with a simple answer, which I share here. It works for me and helps distinguish the Biblical emphasis from all the ideas preached.

The other woman? Don't fear to read about it. Every pastor faces the transference phenomenon in counseling. Many innocent women with no interest beyond the solution to their problem find themselves enamored, and sometimes the pastor has to address such feelings within himself. It is common and not sinful, if it is decisively addressed with Godly wisdom.

Appendix A: Tithing

One issue of ongoing interest to the church is financial giving, tithing to be precise. We preachers have been taught to schedule a yearly sermon underscoring tithing as a law of God that must be obeyed.

The tithe in Malachi's time was promised blessings that—some understand from the language—would exceed their wildest dreams.

> Bring ye all the tithes into the storehouse, that there may be meat in mine house, and prove me now herewith, saith the LORD of hosts, if I will not open you the windows of heaven, and pour you out a blessing, that [there shall] not [be room] enough [to receive it]. (Malachi 3:10)

These blessings, for a materialistic age and a congregation that probably fancies winning the lottery, become a financial thing. No one is interpreting the prophet to mean health or domestic bliss or anything other than more money.

In fact, Jesus' words in Luke's gospel are brought into service here to support the idea that every dollar given is an investment that brings greater financial dividends.

> Give, and it shall be given unto you; good measure, pressed down, and shaken together, and running over, shall men give into your bosom. For with the same measure that ye mete withal it shall be measured to you again. (Luke 6:38)

The plain truth is that this is not the plain truth. When I found opportunity to do a detailed study of the Biblical idea of the tithe, my research took me in a different direction. Luke 6:38 in context is referring to loving your enemies, being merciful and not condemning. But I was in no real position to oppose the common interpretation. All I chose to do was not to preach on the topic, in hopes it would go away.

In practice, I gave money back that was given under false pretense or duress or pressure. On one occasion, it was a $10,000 donation given by a gentleman from the sale of his house. His wife's consternation made her disapproval obvious to us. The trustees promised to pay it back. It was a large sum in those days, and some had been reallocated already, so, payments would be in installments as contributions made it possible. On another occasion, I returned $1,000 which I had rejected because it was given under duress.

If someone came to me with a choice between buying bread or giving to the church, I told them to buy the bread, because I found support in Scripture for fiscal responsibility more immediately applicable and instructive than enriching the church's coffers. In my opinion, the tithe was misappropriated.

I couldn't say this in the pulpit. Church leadership enjoyed having money to spend. Don't we all?

Their fear, I think, is that if we don't remind people of a given truth —and in their minds, tithing qualifies here—the people will soon forget it and lapse into irresponsibility. If we say it is okay not to tithe, just to give as you feel led, they will never feel led. Then the church funds will dry up, and we could be in dire fiscal straits. Besides, the average parishioner would not be relieved to hear that we have been lying to them all these years. Their feelings would begin vacillating between confusion and rage, and that is not what a pastor is called to stir up.

But the truth still remains the truth, and even a cursory study of Scripture should bring others to the same conclusion to which I came.

What is that conclusion? Are you ready for this? It is blatantly clear and irrefutably evident, at least to me.

Simply put, the tithe in Old Testament times was designated for the priests' salaries. This included all full-time temple workers, down to the janitors, who were also part of the same tribe, the Levites.

Deuteronomy 14:22: "You shall surely tithe all the produce from what you sow, which comes out of the field every year."

Numbers 18:26: "Moreover, you shall speak to the Levites and say to them, 'When you take from the sons of Israel the tithe which I have given you from them for your inheritance...'"

If one looks closely at the Scripture on the subject they may, as I did, observe some interesting facts about the narrative. Firstly, they would tithe food, not money. If there needed to be repairs made to the temple, they took special monetary collections, not to be confused at all with the ten percent of their crops and herds that went to the clergy for food and sustenance.

Secondly, Israel in Old-Testament times lived under a theocracy, not a democracy. The government was not taking fifty percent of everything they made. We can put this in Biblical terms of Samuel's concern.

> And he [a king, i.e., the government] will take your
> fields, and your vineyards, and your olive yards, [even]
> the best [of them], and give [them] to his servants. And he
> will take the tenth of your seed, and of your vineyards,
> and give to his officers, and to his servants. (1 Samuel

8:14,15)

Thirdly, there was more than one priest or temple worker per 200 temple goers, probably today's average. The Levites were one of twelve tribes, so the ratio was much tighter. If we were to translate all our tithes into groceries, how much do you think would be too much for the pastor and his family to consume? If we work God's math, it might make a little more sense. The other tribes, compared to the Levites, numbered 11 to 1. The Levites received in effect 110% of the income the other tribes earned. But since the Levites took ten percent of what they got and sacrificed it to God, they were left with 100%, or roughly the same amount of whatever other tribes had. This is assuming that the number of individuals in all tribes was the same and the crop yield was the same. Now, we know this to be highly unlikely, so we concede that point, but God's math still gave the Levites and their families an amount of food comparable to the average. I think we can admit that.

Every third year, a second tithe was taken for the poor. Again, it was food, not money.

> When thou hast made an end of tithing all the tithes
> of your increase the third year, [which is] the year of
> tithing, and hast given [it] unto the Levite, the stranger,
> the fatherless, and the widow, that they may eat within
> thy gates, and be filled. (Deuteronomy 26:12)

This food together with the right to glean in the wheat and barley fields at season's end after the harvest, gave them enough to eat. Homelessness was probably not a problem, since most Israelites inherited part of their parents' estate, and this was perpetual. If they held a mortgage, it was wiped every fifty years.

Beginning to get a different picture? Perhaps. but the tithe is Biblical and can even serve in our time within a Biblical perspective, if we look more closely at it with honest inquiry.

We notice, for one, that the government has taken over many of the responsibilities given to ancient Israel. But then again, it was their government that organized it. They were under a theocracy. God was their ruling body.

It goes without saying that inheritances are not legally protected anymore. There is a tax on it for starters. And if your debt results in a lien upon your house, there is no fifty year parenthesis to help you keep it.

Laying all this aside, my recommendation is to make sure the pastor and his family, if they are full-time, are able to live on a comparable economic level as the average of their congregation. At least provide them with a livable salary. Think of it. If eleven families assume this responsibility, it should work. What happens to the pastor's tithe? I don't care. How about the poor? Or let pastors share in a collective support program for home-missions works.

Comparable should mean that the pastor gets to have a homestead. He should have the church's blessing to own a home. Goodbye vow of poverty, and goodbye parsonages, manses, and so forth. And goodbye private jets and 50-room mansions and condos in Florida, too. But hello to retirement accounts and a reasonable salary.

What about affording the building, the church? What about money for carpets and air conditioners? Church rent or mortgage? And utilities? What about it? It has nothing biblically to do with the tithe. Any money —and this in old Israel was actual money—is collected separately. Again, in Israel, since it was a theocracy, there was a head tax. We cannot relate to it unless we enjoin the government to build our sanctuaries for us. That's not going to happen.

> And thy estimation shall be of the male from twenty
> years old even unto sixty years old, even thy estimation
> shall be fifty shekels of silver, after the shekel of the sanc-
> tuary. (Leviticus 27:3)

Money for rents, mortgages and other nice things for the church are collected separately, or should be.

We obviously have a realistic problem since most people do not tithe as a rule. Furthermore, the pastor's salary is part of an overall budget to support all aspects of the ministry. Some pastors are very well off, because they have large congregations. Others struggle with meeting a home budget. This, in my view, cannot represent the Biblical idea.

The tithe in the New Testament, from the words of Jesus, simply supports His faith as a Jew.

> But woe unto you, Pharisees! for ye tithe mint and
> rue and all manner of herbs, and pass over judgment and
> the love of God: these ought ye to have done, and not to
> leave the other undone. (Luke 11:42)

I have come to believe that tithing has been updated, if not replaced, with Paul's words to the Corinthians. They are self-explanatory for my purpose here.

> Each one {must do} just as he has purposed in his
> heart, not grudgingly or under compulsion, for God loves
> a cheerful giver. (2 Corinthians 9:7)

I am not a debater. My reasoning here is to relate the pain of conscience that this issue has caused me, and I apologize for not resolving it in my experience. Had I, I might have found things a lot easier economically.

Oh, what about TV preachers? If they are worth their salt, designate your offerings to pay for the air time. I do not believe there is any such thing as a TV pastor. They should stick to evangelism.

When it is all boiled down, giving is giving. As long as the figures are disclosed to the givers, and they consent, all is well in Christendom. Even the government is happy with that. So that's that.

Over the past ten years, we have supported a number of ministries. But I doubt that it was ten percent.

Appendix B: In Defense of the Gospel

There are many forgotten sons and daughters, who had grown up in our churches but who have now slipped through the exits and disappeared into our current culture. We did not even see them leave, because we were not looking. Their faith, which may have had a good start, was no longer evident. Dare we say, it was torn from them in the religious mayhem that went on around them. They were too close to the action. While we, the church, argued our doctrines and jostled for the best seat from which to be heard, while we fought on, they became casualties of our friendly fire. It was a religious war we did not even think we were fighting. It was a belligerence that sounded at the time like honest debate or the right thing to do, and we did not think the children were listening.

They were. They heard it all, and they had a far better sense of interpretation than our passion, or enthusiasm, or whatever emotion it was, allowed us to have.

Theologically, this makes no good sense, and that is the point. The so-called logic in our theology appeared logical. It appeared to make a complete circle of reason, but it didn't. We could not see any contradiction in anything we were heralding as truth. While driven by a genuine interest in what we were saying, or some fear of rejection if we didn't, while we passionately defended what we believed, our children beside us silently seemed to disappear into unimportance. As adults, we were determined that nothing would be put above God. God came first.

Are we looking back and reviving our interest in family? Good for us! We should be. It should be obvious to us now that "God first" had been misunderstood. In fact most of our doctrine that is tangential to the theme of Scripture, the salvation plan, is easily misunderstood by others and little known by us who expound it.

The unhappy footnote is that no doctrine is complete or without its mystery. No one has figured out God's mind enough even to begin to understand the basics of faith. That is, perhaps, in part, why they call it faith. But at the time, it made good sense to defend the faith. It may have seemed good that our faith was going strong, faith in terms of our beliefs, our creeds, or whatever we understood the church to believe.

Many of these beliefs that were then important are now never spoken. Some have become mere historical notes, which we may even embarrassingly discard. We do not even remember why they were so meaningful. We can't go into it, let alone get into it, but where is the importance of the one-thousand years now in our homilies? How sure are we now of the when of Messiah's coming? How clear is grace to us that we will anymore vehemently support our own meaning of the term? Grace may be seen as the ability of God's love to provide a way to reconcile us to Himself. He finds the way, even though we would—no, could—never guess how. Someone once said that trying to understand God's grace is like marking out the boundary of a lake, only to discover that we have come to the immeasurable sea.

God's grace and what took place on Golgotha's hill and the Resurrection and faith are pivotal matters. They are eternal issues. They are real to us, historically real, personally real, real in our experience, as real to us as life itself. But we were like the proverbial blind man describing an elephant. We knew the elephant was real, but our explanation of it lacked adequate detail to define or describe it. While we argued that it is like a rope— no like a tree trunk— no... and so forth... no real explanation was ever advanced. Our kids got the theology, but not necessarily the experience; the logic, but not the spirit of the truth.

How do we share this truth with this generation now? They were moved aside in our enthusiasm to advance these beliefs. It is no longer a simple Sunday School lesson or catechism. Our children are young adults. They are college-educated, and some other ideas which make good sense to them have captured their attention instead.

Can we reach any of them? Do they know that God still loves them? Do they even know or imagine that there is a God out there? That's a more fundamental belief lost in college textbooks, the electronic age, and scientific advancement.

What can we say to them now that can argue for their right to believe in God? What line of reasoning or logic can begin with their understanding of things, their base of knowledge, what is important to them, and then take just one small step in God's direction?

They are aspiring scientists, after a sort.

To say that faith has nothing to do with science is to say that science has nothing to do with faith, and that is not only ignoring a major part of the spirit of scientific inquiry, but more to the point here, it closes the door on all opportunity to talk to this forgotten generation. We cannot argue science wrong. It has come of age and is the language of reason for today. We are not privileged even in the name of God's authority to discredit it and hope to win any point of logic. If we want to relate to our children, if we want to talk to them, adult to adult, and tell them anything that is important to us, we must not put ourselves at odds with what they in our absence have come to accept as the true approach to learning.

One of our greatest arguments is from history, since history is a major part of any serious proof. But history has disappointed us. We rightly maintain that the Resurrection of Christ from the dead is a proven historical event, and on this depends all faith. But history is interpreted, and furthermore, we cannot use head-knowledge necessarily to instill heart-knowledge.

Miracles, also, performed by God and God's means of revealing His presence, are often lost in the haystack of coincidence and inevitability.

Arguments aside, is there still a God out there that loves them and would like a chance to show it?

Let's start with some apologies. It is still okay to say that we're sorry. We lost sight of the Christ in our Christianity. We were sure that we needed to defend the Church's beliefs against those who would argue them wrong. But the church needed no defense. It's still thriving. That was a prophecy that stands or falls on its own merit.

Do we love them? How can we make that patently clear to them?

Can the Christ in us, unknown to them, begin to care? Can we take all those beautiful, heartfelt, Pharisaic principles that make such good sermon material and, setting them aside for the moment (or maybe for good) visit this generation?

If Jesus visited abused women or tax collectors, how much more sense does it make for us to make time for our forgotten children?

Don't talk theology. We have to find a way to show it, if it is real. We need to just live our faith out in front of them without saying a word about it.

"But they smoke, drink, swear, and watch adult movies."

"But I cannot endorse drugs, or children out of wedlock."

"Do you have any idea who they are living with?"

"They have rings and tattoos all over them."

Whatever!

Is there light in us that can overcome whatever we perceive as darkness? Then let it shine.

"But they don't want us around!"

So? When has that stopped us before? When we fought in our churches in front of their then-formative and impressionable minds and hearts, we fought with people who didn't want us around. Did we leave? Did they? The fighting would have stopped.

We need to talk their language. Skip the clichés. (They don't mean anything to them, anyhow.) We must find a way of saying what we want to say in terms they may listen to. Granted, we enjoy our Christian songs and all the inspiring phrases sung. We sit with eyes closed and dream about our absent children listening to this one or that one. We wish there was a way to take the messages in song that so move us to prayer and have our kids hear them.

Let it go.

It cannot be done? Not so! But we need to somehow move aside and let God show Himself, if He will. We need to apologize. Given a second opportunity in some future ministry or church, we need to get it right for the next generation of youth, who have a right to the truth.

There, I said it and it feels good.

Appendix C: What is Christianity?

The Bible is actually simple. The message is simple. What makes Christianity what it is, or what defines it, is simple. It is one idea, which I am convinced has to be unique among thinkers, since it is first presented in the Bible. The idea of God dying was not unique, though it was uncommon in the writers and thinkers of antiquity. However, the idea that God, any god, would take punishment meant for someone else was totally foreign. Dr. Gregory Boyd, a professor at Bethel College, St. Paul, Minnesota, concurred:

> There is no other belief which does this... Only the Gospel dares to proclaim that God enters smack-dab into the middle of the hell we created. Only the Gospel dares to proclaim that God was born a baby in a bloody, crap-filled stable, that He lived a life befriending the prostitutes and lepers no one else would befriend, and that He suffered firsthand, the hellish depth of all that is nightmarish in human existence.

The idea? God, in the person of someone named Jesus Christ, took on Himself the punishment for our sins. The Greek philosophers and the great thinkers of ancient civilizations never wrote about it, and that is important to me.

A unique idea begs the question of its origin. William F. Albright, called the father of Biblical archeology, in his dissertation, "From the Stone Age to Christianity," shows—at least to my ignorance—that monotheism, a belief in one God, comes from Moses on Mount Sinai. If you are Jewish, you should be excited to hear this. You might also take an immediate interest in it if you are a Christian. Albright is now argued to be unscientific, and you can easily find anthropological studies of Middle Eastern civilizations that do not see it this way. But for a Christian, this one and only God is big and has become God's self-introduction to us for reasons that involve the ministry and death of His son, Jesus Christ.

The Christian or Christ-idea comes in five parts, where the first one, the leading idea, presents the other four.

The foremost idea is that Jesus the Christ was put to death on a Roman cross for a crime he did not commit. In this case, capital punishment was not a mistake, but in God's mind, we maintain, he paid the penalty for sins or crimes against God that we committed. We called this "the vicarious atonement." Okay. I can accept that phrase. In order to support this simple but mysterious idea, four other doctrines—if I may call them doctrines—came about.

One, since this idea is in the Bible, this book must be God's book. He must be the author of it. This led many to maintain that consequently, each word in a Biblical idea has to have been picked by God personally, and the very languages the Bible was originally written in became grammatically significant, in order to obtain the exact meaning of truth.

Two, if this Jesus were just a man, or only human, legally speaking, he could not meet the punishment, since one man can only except the punishment for one other, not for everyone. This reasoning may or may not be accurate, but Christians came to believe from a closer look at the Bible that this Jesus was definitely more than human. We say, He is also divine, and He is the only one.

If this is true, thirdly, Mary, his mother, must have become pregnant with him before she was married. She was a virgin, and some say she remained so, an idea not immediately necessary to support the idea that God in the person of Christ died for all.

Fourth, we faced the issue that if Jesus was divine, and so, was God, was there more than one? We remained grateful to Judaism for maintaining that there is only one God. This led to the belief in the Trinity, that there is only one God, but in three persons. The explanation has proved somewhat difficult to come up with. Dr. Boyd said, "We can't conceive how it is true, but there are good grounds for believing that it is true." The third person is the Holy Spirit, which we added because He is mentioned in the Bible all over the place.

If you buy these, actually, if you accept the first one, the vicarious atonement, even if you cannot explain it, you are a Christian. Dorothy Sayers, in her play Man Born to Be King, has Mary the mother of Jesus looking up at him on the cross and saying, "From the beginning of history until now, this is the only thing that as ever really happened."

I don't intend to get preachy. I would have written this differently if it were meant to be a sermon. I needed to present first the plain and simple idea that distinguishes Christianity from all other religions before I could go on.

If you are scientific, you begin to have a real problem with this definition of Christianity. How does a virgin get pregnant?

"Larry King made a very perceptive comment," says Ravi Zacharias in Can Man Live without God, "when he was asked who he would most like to have interviewed from across history. One of those he named was

Jesus Christ... 'I would like to ask him,' [said Larry,] 'if he was indeed virgin born...' Larry King was absolutely right in identifying the hinge upon which all history turns."

What can it possibly mean when Christianity talks about three persons in one, or Jesus as an historical figure having two natures, being both God and man. The biggest problem is trying to figure out how anyone's murder or assassination could translate into my friendship with God. These questions can be asked if I get by the problem of believing that there is such a God that would care about being my friend.

I may make a few preachers angry by saying so, but you may have a real claim here. If we look closely at Scripture, nowhere is the Trinity, three-in-one, specifically and clearly stated. There is one Scripture that said it, but it was found to have been edited to say that much later. This is an honest contribution from scholarship.

Even the word nature, used to describe Jesus as having two of them, was stated in Latin, not in the original Bible language.

Many also struggle with the New Testament as being God's Word, since there are over 250,000 variations among all the different copies in the so-called original language. Why hide this from you? There are a few Old Testament text differences as well, although the scribes who made copies of it were admittedly very careful.

Good news: none of these variants calls into question the vicarious atonement in the New Testament. The Old Testament struggled with the idea of Christ the innocent One dying for someone else. This idea of substitution was not easily said in their language, but the message was that God was real and personable, and the Prophet Isaiah only introduced this great New Testament theme in his 53rd chapter. We are back where we started in defining what Christianity should be all about.

Dorothy Sayers, in Creed or Chaos , summarized thusly:

> So that is the outline of the official story—the talk of
> the time when God was the underdog and got beaten,
> when he submitted to the conditions he had laid down
> and became a man like the men he had made, and the
> men he had made broke him and killed him.

So it seems that Christianity started with a unique idea which could be described (Jesus on the Cross) but not explained. Then we proceeded to tie up logical loose ends with four other ideas that are somewhat challenging to prove.

One good thing to remember is that this is it. There is no other doctrine or idea or philosophy that needs to be thrown into this discussion.

Science, if you want to use science here, need not prove anything else at all. But for the record, I believe it with my whole heart.

Appendix D: The Other Woman

Some years after your Grandpa King died, your Aunt Faith asked me if it was true that he had had a girlfriend. Her question had to be a painful inquiry. It took her years, evidently, to muster the resolve to get by her natural desire to forget about it. We all have such hurtful thoughts, which we try to suppress or disown. But apparently, Aunt Faith could not bury the question. The winds of hurtful memories continued to blow over the shallow grave of a family history that she could not forget. It was once again on her mind. What she knew, or thought she knew, about our dad didn't seem to be all pieces of the same puzzle. She asked me, one day, straight up, did dad have a girlfriend, and I told her, "No!" And I really meant, no. I didn't just make up an answer she wanted to hear, although I am quite sure that it is what she wanted to hear.

I could also understand how such a rumor could have found a life of its own, once started. The weeds of gossip grow fast.

Grandpa King, word had it, had a separate savings account which Grandma King knew nothing about until after his death, and the account was brought to light with a zero balance. I am not sure of the particulars, but my mom was sure my dad had had it for another woman.

Other women were indeed available for a waiter in the 1950's. It was not unexpected for dad working in room service to find in an open doorway a woman in lingerie, or less. And such a woman had occasionally wanted him to join her. Grandpa worked with women as well, and some of them were quite frisky, no doubt.

I took a walk with my dad one day, upon his request, and he shared with me his challenge and his innocence. If you had met your Grandpa King, you like me would have had no trouble believing him outright.

What was the bank account all about? I could only guess, but I knew Grandpa worried about money. One day we were discussing money interests in a normal voice, and two rooms away, Grandpa was supposedly asleep. I can't remember what it was we wanted to buy. Dad could sleep through all kinds of childhood noise, but talk money even in a whisper, and he would hear it. From the bedroom off the dining room came his voice, "Do you kids think money grows on trees?!" He also carried around a little black book of figures and a pencil with which to constantly rework them.

On our walk, he expressed his frustration and regret over my mom's inheritance of $1,600 upon the death of her brother, my uncle Al. Mom

175

bought wall-to-wall carpeting for the living room and hallway and the stairway heading to the second floor, instead of paying bills. When it came to spending money, my parents were not on the same wavelength. In fact, at times, they were totally out of phase. I think if Grandpa experimented with another account, he did it to exercise some financial independence, to mitigate his worry.

None of this suggests that I think any less of my dad. I don't. I miss him. I do not assume for an instant that anything other than what I just stated ever happened. We were one big happy family, and I mean happy. I knew through my childhood that I was loved. I was spoiled that way.

I have learned that somehow if a married man has a friend who is another woman, it has to be sexual and wrong. Well, if it is sexual, it is wrong. But if a married woman has a male friend which is non-sexual, it is okay. We may need to rethink all of this.

It is true that such friendships blur relationships, since relationships are defined by the degree of intimacy they represent. Intimacy is not necessarily sexual, of course. It could be simply sharing one's troubles at what otherwise appears a legitimate business luncheon. People have been crossing back and forth past this blurred line for generations. That is what I believe I have learned by observing my own parents and their relationships.

We learn where that line is by crossing it. We sometimes sense that we have shared too much with the wrong person only after we have shared it. We sometimes catch ourselves enjoying someone's company a little too much. It was as if a childhood romance which had to be innocent by definition snuck up on us unawares. Perhaps we foolishly thought we knew where the line was, and thought we could come to it without crossing over. Bad idea.

As a pastor, I counseled individuals to help them identify not merely the line but where they stood in relation to it and what direction they were heading in. Life is never so simple that people are going to admit where they are and where they're heading. Some backed off and went home to family. Some did not. They crossed the line and kept on going over the horizon and out of the sight of the very people they once loved. That's sad.

This is not some kind of text on marriage counseling. These comments were intended to show you part of my pastoral world that wasn't evident to you while you were growing up.

It is something called transference.

Sigmund Freud first identified the psychological pro-

cess of transference and brought it into what is now modern day psychotherapy. As a therapist he noticed that
people had strong feelings and fantasies about him that
had no basis in reality. But Freud died before there was
such a thing as "rock and roll." Transference has become
a more modern concept since Freud. In fact, many people
believe transference is actually something that happens in
life—and not just psychotherapy... Transference can
sometimes produce a powerful love or a destructive ha-
tred based on a complete illusion... (Michael G. Conner,
Psy.D)

I was not told about this in Bible school. I discovered in ministry and
in life that there was such a dynamic and that it could be troublesome at
best. I eventually learned to recognize the signs in a counselee and make
a quick referral to another counselor, but until then I was dealing with it
in my own, fumbling way.

These persons become emotionally very vulnerable, and the pastor,
very powerful. I think a clergyman could do as he willed with them, no
questions asked. It most likely would have become a fatal attraction—if
you've seen the movie—and that does happen to some clergy. The clergy
appears the victim caught in the black widow's web, but in reality, he is
the one in control, and he lost it. They call this counter-transference.

Now, I do not know how many such relationships—or fantasies is a
more appropriate term—I had avoided over the years. Only a couple examples come briefly to mind, and I am not even sure they are good examples of this phenomenon.

With all the problems Mom and I were facing in our young marriage
of only 4 years, we didn't need Suzie (not her real name). The exact role
Suzie played in all of our woes is not clear. It may be my naiveté talking,
but to this day I have unanswered questions, and I am sure Mom would
be happy to leave them unanswered.

We lived in Butler during the trying years 1971-72. Some pieces to
this Butler puzzle were missing until the school's former president
showed up one day in 1988 in Norwood, MA and told me that Suzie had
died of a cancerous brain tumor. I will explain shortly, but for now, i was
interesting to learn this, years after it had happened.

Who was Suzie? Suzie was a pretty young student at the school,
who took a keen interest in every class I taught: English, Greek, and even
classical Hebrew. When I would arrive early at the school to have breakfast with the students before class, Suzie somehow knew I had arrived,

though unannounced, time and again, and toasted me a Thomas' English muffin. The school had a truckload of the things, because they had been given as a donation.

The school board, realizing my financial crisis, gave me a job painting the parsonage where the school president and his family lived. He told me to ask the students to help. It wasn't against the rules, and it wasn't my idea, so, I put out a broadcast for help. You guessed it: Suzie showed up, and she was the only one who showed up.

Did I mention I was naive as well as stupid?

One day when she sat across from me at the lunch table at school—it was lunchtime for all students—it finally dawned on me that this was not right, so I put a stop to it.

How? I introduced Suzie to a handsome young student who would later become her husband, and knowing that Mom and I had our domestic problems, I simply went home to talk. That was a good idea, since I did then as I do now: I love your mother.

At first, I wondered why the president told me in 1988 that she had died. I came up with this answer: the school board must have concluded with so much Suzie in my school life, something must have been happening. This might explain why, when a full time position opened at the school, the board did not give it to me but to the new man, who was in my opinion far less qualified.

Suzie was nothing more than one of my students. I don't know how to say it more definitively so that my response is clear. Please see her as only that. That's how involved I was with her on a personal level.

Did I enjoy this uncommon attention? Yes, briefly, until the effects of the naiveté pill wore off at that lunch table one day.

I did learn one thing. What appears as innocent interaction can be, if not stopped, a dangerous time at play. It is like horsing around, splashing childlike in a pool of water, deep water and we are about to drown.

There will from time to time be a Suzie in every minister's life. There is no bad person here. This is simply a relationship that threatens to veer off the main path and go in the wrong direction. Most of the time, a pastor and his counselee, or a teacher and his student, know this and prevent any mistake. Emotions do not always cooperate. That's why God gave us brains along with them.

Perhaps the only thing to care about here is that Mom and I are still together and still in love.

Appendix E: Closing Defense

Writing about the years we were in ministry is not without its risk at exposing me as someone between incompetent and just plain bad. The reason for this risk exists, because my purpose in this writing was to provoke self-evaluation and at the same time speak ill of no one. I do this not only for my own benefit, but also as a teacher, who by example wants to take some leadership to encourage the same in you.

The obvious fact is that everyone has a continuing need for self-reevaluation. Everyone should reassess their actions and their achievements in terms of their life goals. Everyone should be the first to come down hard on himself for wrongs he knows he has committed, and after knocking himself down, should be the first to pick himself back up and go forward a different person. Saint Paul in the Bible referred to this as keeping his body in subjection. Interesting phrase. Everyone needs to get tough with himself from time to time, repent if necessary, and then move on. I am talking here about ordinary people, good people who because of the human condition are capable of making mistakes.

So, back to me, what can I say in my defense? How do I get my life back from what appears to be 25 years of a failed experiment in pastoring? I already advanced the argument that as a teacher I accomplished a few good things. Also, pioneering a new thought, I concluded, I along with many in my generation helped clear a path to a new Church.

I mentioned you, my family. I could go through a hurricane with you, and because you were with me, the experience would be all it was advertised to be. I could look back on it as an exciting ride, an adrenaline high, a breathtaking adventure.

But is this enough to salvage the past? My melancholia and my tendency to withdraw from emotional pain, rather than take it on, my desire at times to see other people have a chance at success, sometimes at the price of my own, and finding it difficult on occasion to confront people when I thought they needed to reconsider their actions, because I knew such a thought would pain them, all these lead to an impression of failed leadership.

But no one's life is a failure. I have said that of others, and now I must say that of myself, and here is why.

It is worth repeating that life is worth living, if along the way you experience peaks of achieving personal goals that stretched your capabilities beyond your expectations. I have had these. There have a been a few

179

septic tanks in my life that I have had to dig around. Probably the biggest was the career-change. I look back almost in disbelief that we did it. That has to say something good about me.

Life is worth it, if you can look back on family moments that remind you that you are loved and that you are a vital part of what makes them someone you can be proud of. In my case, I have you, my three sons, all of whom I can be proud. Can I claim a small, small piece of your successes?

Life is not a total wreck for me, since I can say that I remain in love with and married to the same woman for 40-plus years. What about that?

Let's talk in general. Ultimately, when someone looks back on his life, a sense of failure is not determined by how much pain he's experienced or how many times he's had to pick himself up again after a mistake. Personal success or failure is not determined either by what other people might think of him. It all boils down to how he measures meaningfulness in his existence. Did he reach for the moon but found it too distant to touch? Perhaps, but he was able to grab hold of a life experience that was within his reach but appeared a stretch.

Speaking of myself, 25 years of ministry did touch many lives in a very positive way. Many people who needed us found us nearby and ready to help. The lives we touched never made the statistics. No one else may have known how these people benefited from knowing us. But we knew.

I did not take the space here to boast about achievements or peak moments when someone's life was put back on track or helped in someway because he knew me, but it happened over and over and over again.

I sat before boards that argued denominational privilege or organizational growth, while all I could care about was one more very private soul discovering the secret to living with conflict or the secret to escaping some temptation that held them.

Professionally, I was paid perhaps to command crowds, but all I wanted to do was visit one more person and help them live above their pain. I never saw numbers. I saw only individual persons, whose lives like the snowflakes were unique. I could not preach some patented solution to their problems. I needed to care on a personal level, and if that meant minimizing the importance of corporate projects and corporate programs, I did it intentionally.

Yes, in some regards, we are all alike. We are all human, and I guess we can be categorized on some level as men and women with needs peculiar to our species and gender, but that is not enough for a pastor who cares about people. On some level of need, personality, and abilities, each of us is very different from everyone else.

I made a life as a pastor trying to help people discover biblical solutions for their unique situations. If they had that solution in common with another, it only proved the benefit of Scripture. It was never a reason to formulate another theology or pass out an interpretation of some Truth to fit all needs.

I enjoyed studying Scripture and discussing with others what I thought I'd found. Together, we might discover something of value to our own interests in life and as Christians.

Let's do it again!

Part-Time Custodian Resigns To Become Full-Time Teacher

No one seeing custodian John King sweep the floors at Connoquenessing School would guess that Biblical Greek and Hebrew are his "favorite subjects."

An opportunity to teach these subjects brought King from New Jersey to Butler in late summer of 1971. A similar opportunity will move him and his family to Washington later this year. The part-time custodian for Butler Area Schools has resigned to accept a full-time teaching position beginning Nov. 24 at Lighthouse Faith Bible School in Washington.

King began his education at State University of New York in Buffalo, his hometown. He spent two years majoring in chemistry with a math minor and "heading for a job in bio-chemistry research." But soon the direction changed.

He entered Northeast Bible Institute, now Northeast Bible College, near Philadelphia. "That's where I picked up Greek and Hebrew," he explains. In 1963, after four years of study, he received a diploma which qualified him to accept an Assembly of God pastorate.

A licensed minister for that denomination, King received his license from a credentials committee, "basically an examination board," after a series of interviews, oral and written exams, and a review of his record.

Licensing, he explains, gives a minister the authority to perform a marriage ceremony and other church services and functions. It is dependent on the possibility of a pastorate, an indication to the committee of the applicant's seriousness of purpose.

After serving two years as pastor of an Assembly of God church in West Cape May, N.J., King came to Butler in 1971 to teach his "favorite subjects," Biblical Greek and Hebrew, at Western Pennsylvania Bible Institute located now on Route 422 west at Parvis Road. The Rev. Hubert G. Benney is minister of the Assembly of God church and president of the institute, both part of the complex.

The teaching assignment was part-time, and in December, 1972 King joined the custodial staff of the Butler Area Schools "to supplement my income." He admits that scrubbing pots and pans in the kitchen to work his way through Northeast Bible Institute was the "closest I'd come to custodial work" before joining the Butler staff.

His first custodial job was at Bon Aire School, but he has also worked at Meridian, Center Avenue, and the intermediate high school on either a full-time or part-time basis.

"As my teaching ministry grew, I had to cut back on custodial work," says King. He has worked part-time at Connoquenessing since mid-May of this year. It is his second assignment at that particular school.

His 3-7 p.m. shift follows a day of teaching which begins between 8 and 9 a.m. and ends by 2:30 p.m.

Reviewing his education, King admits, "I loved chemistry, still do. I loved the chemistry lab." Greek, on the other hand, is "a profession, a hobby, and everything else."

King and his family will move to Washington later this year from their home on McCandless Drive in Center Township. He married his wife, Joyce, while they were both students at Northeast Bible Institute. Their sons are James, 2, and Timmy, 6, a first grader at Center Township School.

At Lighthouse Faith Bible School he is scheduled to teach Biblical Greek, New Testament books, particularly the Pauline epistles, and Reformation theology. The emphasis in Greek is on translation, not on speaking the language. The Washington school is "more on the institute level," says King. Only the Bible is taught.

A man who keeps setting goals for himself, King has applied for a Bachelor of Science degree credit based on his work at SUNY and Northeast Bible Institute. He wants to go back to school. The master's degree program in philosophy at W and J College in Washington is one possibility.

But most of all, he says, "I'd like to write a book." King has already chosen the title. A

CHANGING ROLES — John King, a part-time custodian at Connoquenessing School, enjoys a chapter of Hebrew during his work break. An opportunity to teach Biblical Greek and Hebrew at Western Pennsylvania Bible Institute brought King from New Jersey to Butler in late summer of 1971. A similar opportunity will move him and his family to Washington later this year. The part-time custodian has resigned to accept a full-time teaching position beginning Nov. 24 at Lighthouse Faith Bible School in Washington.

Butler Eagle photo

West Cape May, NJ

Burgettstown, PA

Norwood, MA

Our First Apartment, Green Lane, PA

West Street, Butler, PA
McCandless Drive, Butler, PA

Shady Ave, Burgettstown, PA

Mom & Dad holding Josh
Front: James and Tim

Earl Adams

Daisy McGill

Shorty (Ralph) & Mary Ellen Camp

Left to Right: Amy & Denny Thompson,   Nick & Trish
Me, Jan & Gary Davis   Langione

Pastor & Nadine VanRiper

Booth's Algorithm: My Lab Project at FSC

Bonsai: My Shell Beach in MA.

My Three Sons and
Joyce & Me when young and naive

Printed in the United States
205303BV00001B/370-405/P